Radical Perceptions

Brilliant Thoughts
For an Amazing Life

by Graham Cooke

The Wisdom Series — Book Two

Brilliant
BOOK HOUSE

www.BrilliantBookHouse.com

Wisdom that stretches our thinking and enlarges our heart.

A book of aphorisms by Graham Cooke.

Brilliant Book House LLC
865 Cotting Ln, Ste C
Vacaville, California 95688
U.S.A.

www.brilliantbookhouse.com

© 2011 Graham Cooke

Unless otherwise indicated, all Scripture quotations are taken from The Holy Bible, New King James Version (Copyright © 1979, 1980, 1982 by Thomas Nelson, Inc.) and the New American Standard Bible (Copyright © 1960, 1962, 1963, 1971, 1972, 1973, 1975, 1977, 1995 by The Lockman Foundation).

Requests for information should be addressed to:

Graham Cooke

office@myemerginglight.com

ISBN: 978-1-934771-22-8

Dedication

I devote this book to members of The Warrior Class. This is a community of Prophetic Intercessors who support the assignments around my ministry through prayer, prophetic perception and military intelligence.

Together we seek to produce breakthrough in whatever place the Lord commands us to go. The Warrior Class are people who are devoted to training, learning and their own development. They are fighters, warriors and champions in the Joshua and Caleb mold.

They love intimate connection with the Lord Jesus and adore Life in the Holy Spirit. They are a great crew.

I especially dedicate this book to Allison Bown, the Director of The Warrior Class and the Council that support her in leadership. This team plus the Regional Leaders who provide oversight and support on the ground all have my thanks for the sterling work they provide in ensuring that every event I do has a strong, powerful, prophetic edge.

We can't all get it together; but together we can get it all.

Graham

For more information on the Warrior Class visit www.GrahamCooke.com.

Acknowledgements

I love people who make me think. I especially love people who can say a lot with few words. Bill Johnson, Lance Wallnau, Steve Witt, Karen Thrall, David Crabtree, Gerald Coates, Dan McCollam, Tony Morton, Jim McNeish, Bob Book, Rachel Hickson, Bob Mumford, Roger Ellis, Martin Scott and Graham Perrins. They have all played a part in my life and development.

A Note on Meditation

The purpose of this book is to lead you out of the busyness of life and into the still waters of deep thought, restful perception and therefore *presence*. As you give yourself to this process you will become more God-conscious, more of a worshipper, and more peaceful in how you approach life.

To meditate means to think deeply about something or someone. It means to explore with mind and heart, allowing what you think to touch your innermost being.

Meditation is creative thought which leads us to the higher realm of revelation and wisdom. It takes us beyond the place of reason to where joy is seated and faith is activated.

Meditation allows us to search inside and outside the box of our current paradigm. What you see and hear there touches you profoundly. It adds a ring around the core truth of Christ which is God within, the certainty of freedom.

Fruitful meditation is therefore not a casual seeking for revelatory insight. Initial creative thoughts are merely the "X" that marks the spot. There is treasure in meditation, a guarantee of wealth in the pursuit of God.

Many are satisfied with collecting random truth on the surface of their consciousness. It is good, wholesome stuff, but it does not satisfy and it cannot challenge the complexities of life in a warfare context.

Deep truth has to be mined over days and weeks. It takes joy and patience to take truth down to its deepest level. Beyond meeting our current needs. Beyond the depth of understanding the power it releases to us against our adversary. Down to the depth where God lives in the highest places of heaven. For all meditation must ultimately come before the throne of His majesty, sovereignty and supremacy. He fills all things with Himself.

Our current situation requires wisdom, but even more it yearns for *Presence*. Meditation allows us to experience both, through the word coming alive in our spirit. Meditation leads us to God and the permission of His heart. Learn to be in the question peacefully with God. Let the Holy Spirit teach you how to abide. Turn inwardly and rest; wait patiently… He will come. When your heart gets restless, turn to worship. When the interior atmosphere settles, return to listening.

Write down initial thoughts but do not pursue them just yet. Do not be distracted by what you hear initially. Set it aside; come back to it later.

When first entering a lifestyle of meditation, take care to ease into it slowly. An hour at first, then longer until half a day and so on.

Always have a focus; do not try to wait in a vacuum. In this book are a series of sayings and life statements. Take time to process them. Enjoy the stillness of deep thinking and allow your heart to flow in and out of worship.

Use the questions as the Spirit leads. They are not prescriptive but merely a guide to enable your contemplation. No doubt you will discover better questions as the Holy Spirit tutors you.

Enjoy!

About Personal Notes

Following every entry, you will find blank or mostly blank pages like this one. Each of these has a question or questions to help direct you in your meditation. They can be used or ignored; they are merely there as a starting point or guide. These "Personal Notes" sections have been included so you may write His thoughts and keep them close.

Dear Reader:
I have deliberately not
expounded on some
concepts... the Holy
Spirit will have that
pleasure Himself.
Just ask!

We are defined by the quality of the opposition against us!

When we look at a giant, there are mixed messages that we receive. Firstly, the enemy tells us that we are too small and not strong enough, big enough or powerful enough to overcome the opposition in front of us. The purpose of the enemy is to make us feel like grasshoppers in our own sight (Numbers 13:33). The enemy has a vested interest in our low self-esteem and powerlessness.

The Holy Spirit, on the other hand, is always too confident to be taken in by such immature foolishness. He points to the opposition and says: "That's the size you are going to be when this fight is over! By the time we are finished with him you will have exchanged dimension, stature and power. The reason I have given you an enemy of this size and power is so that you will have a visual image of what you are about to become".

As we look at the size of the opposition there is a stirring in our hearts. Destiny always shows its face at moments like this. Joshua became leader of Israel after his encounter with giants. Caleb was rightly called "a man of a different spirit". The enemy always shows you what you must become in order to defeat him. It is part of his unconscious programming and one of the many reasons why God always leads us in triumph (2 Corinthians 2:14).

Our vision of God can never be diminished by the enemy, only enhanced. When we see God as big as He is then our vision of ourselves grows by being in His shadow.

Never take any cue from what the enemy is saying or doing. Our life is only about the power of the one, with the ONE! To overcome we must rethink our status. God allows in His wisdom what He can easily prevent by His power. If we have a giant in our life it is because we are meant to be a giant ourselves. The circumstances in front of us are designed therefore to increase our size in the Spirit.

We are heading into a situation that is suppose to take us to the next dimension of anointing; upgrade our stature in relation to Jesus; and radically increase our power in the Holy Spirit.

Or, if you prefer, you can quit. Go back to Egypt and never realize your true self and the inheritance that goes with it.

Personal Notes

What is the giant in front of you at this time? Describe it and the effect it has on your faith and vision of yourself.

What is the Holy Spirit saying to you through this? What new vision of yourself is forming in your heart? Describe the upgrade.

What promises are coming to this new identity; what provisions and resources can be claimed at this time?

The battle is not ours to win... it is ours to lose

Jesus has disarmed both rulers and authorities, making a mockery of their power in the process and celebrating His own triumph over them by the cross (Colossians 2:15). Now as ever the battle is not ours but the Lord's (2 Chronicles 20:15).

We serve a powerful King who loves to fight! He laughs at those who oppose him (Psalms 2:4; 37:13). In the Kingdom, we fight *from* victory; not towards it. Jesus has already won. In Him we partake of His overcoming. We are more than conquerors because we know the outcome before we enter the fray.

In Christ, our posture before the enemy must reflect our status in the Kingdom. We are an heir of God and a joint heir with Christ. We have been given power and authority through the Holy Spirit. In warfare, we rejoice before we pray. We give thanks for His majesty and supremacy. We are not overcome by our circumstances, we are overwhelmed by sovereignty. We are too busy being fascinated by Jesus to be intimidated by the enemy. We rejoice so that our praying can be powerful and effective. We praise because we occupy the position of an overcomer.

We stand in this space and we occupy our standing in Jesus through praise of His Majesty. The battle is won already; it is our partnering with victory that guarantees the outcome. We have the capacity to lose this battle only by default.

Lack of true rejoicing and thanksgiving will always embolden the enemy at our expense. The power of wickedness may increase in our perception if our worship is diminished and our focus on sovereignty reduced.

The only viable answer to intimidation is an increase in intimacy with the Lord. David was a "man after God's own heart;" i.e., a worshipper. His intimacy gave him power over the intimidation of Goliath. He became a giant killer.

We can lose every fight if we have no focus. If our lives display a lack of worship we will never even show up for the fight. We will lose because we do not know how to stand. We will petition God for power when He has already given us authority in Jesus' name. In rejoicing we receive revelation concerning the particulars of our overcoming.

Decide who you want to be and the Holy Spirit will empower you to become it.

Personal Notes

What victory belongs to you in this current situation?

What upgrade in rejoicing is required?

What position is available to you in Christ at this time?

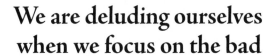

We are deluding ourselves when we focus on the bad

Focus must always empower. It captures our heart and claims our attention. Focus has no preference of its own. It is given one by the disposition of our heart.

No one is born a pessimist. We learn it in the settings of our childhood and from the people who influence us the most. It is a learned behavior that can be unlearned. It is for freedom that Christ has set us free. The world declares a pessimist to be a realist, and an optimist to be an idealist. The Kingdom rightly denounces such nonsense. "As a man thinks in his heart, so is he" (Proverbs 23:7).

In the mind of Christ we can change our perceptions and think better thoughts. Our mind is always renewed by the Spirit. Transformation is available to us in the person of Jesus and the work of the Holy Spirit. In Christ our focus is made glorious by the renewal of the Spirit within. We are no longer made disillusioned by our circumstances or experiences. We can exchange them for better ones. We are never more than a step or two away from an upgrade.

If a million people say a wrong thing, it is still a wrong thing. Jesus is the one voice against many, but His words and perceptions carry more weight than the entire population of this planet. It is the object of our focus that has most power over us. When we focus on a negative, we allow its power into our lives. It shapes us by stripping away our joy, pleasure and comfort. It denies us present and future courage. It renders us powerless today and tomorrow. We are reduced, diminished and defenseless against the circumstances of life. We become deluded and bitter when we do not seek the company of joyful people.

Our biggest delusion perhaps is that one day we can get around to changing our mindset and that our current negativity is not really that harmful. A mindset cannot be changed; it must be replaced. Repentance and obedience is the only way that our delusion can be overcome.

Personal Notes

What is the state of your current focus?

Take a poll of your family and friends. Ask them to comment and give any advice without revealing their identity.

Then? Do what seems good to you and the Holy Spirit.

The "Why" question will never be answered on earth

"Why me?" "Why this?" "Why now?" "Why?!" Often this type of question can come out of shock, anger, self pity and bewilderment. We seek meaning, purpose and significance. This particular question "why?" can deliver none of the answers that would be most helpful. It's the question that will leave us trapped in our own grief and misery. It prevents us from moving on. It creates an inertia in our soul and we remain stuck in a moment in time, unable to extricate our emotions. I have seen those moments of grief become despair, self pity, anger, resentment and bitterness. The heart is overwhelmed and we disappear into ourselves and lose the life we could have enjoyed.

I adored my brother Ian. He died in 1975, at age 26. He was walking to work on an icy canal path one freezing winter morning in the north of England. He slipped on a patch of ice, fell on his head, became unconscious, slid into the water, and drowned. He left a young wife and two small daughters. My heart seemed to freeze in my chest. Our whole family was locked in a grief so despairing we were speechless, adrift in shock. I have never known such awful silence. The "why" question was on all our lips, reducing our capacity to think, squeezing our hearts with its iron grip, numbing us from any other emotion, robbing us of life and purpose.

An answer never came. Some people still ask that same question. They are stuck in the present–past. Life eventually moved on and they moved with it, but a part of their heart is stuck in that moment.

"Everything works together for good..." (Romans 8:28). God does not engineer bad circumstances so that He can produce good, like a rabbit out of a hat. Rather, He knows that on days life has a capacity to be awful and terrible. In those moments He works within us, around us and often through us to bring about some form of release and blessing. Goodness is part of His Truth, His Nature, His Persona.

Traveling north for the funeral I felt too numb even to pray. A scripture was doing the rounds in my head, like a toy train on a loop track. "Rejoice always, in everything give thanks, this is the will of God" (1 Thessalonians 5:16–18). When we cannot pray without ceasing, it's because we have not given thanks enough. I worshipped the whole way home, six hours on two trains and a bus journey to the house of my childhood. I walked into a room frozen with grief, the icicles of despair hanging in the atmosphere, eyes red from crying, family members stumbling around, impotent in their own tragedy.

That night I had a dream. Short, simple, and powerful. It was two men walking up a hill. I could see their backs, not their faces. The whole landscape was a riot of color. Flowers of every shade of brightness grew profusely. It was a warm, sunny day; the sky a perfect blue. The two men were laughing, pulling and pushing on one another. Two friends sharing something hilarious. I wanted to run to catch up with them and share in their moment. At the top of the hill one of the men stopped and turned. Jesus looked at me with that slow gentle smile of His that lights up His whole face. I smiled back. The other man turned and it was my brother. Ian grinned at me in that same, mischievous grin that I knew so well. My heart felt like it was coming out of my chest. We looked at each other and… he winked. With that wink of his eye, strength came back into me.

The next morning I told my family the dream. No one spoke afterwards, but the icicles of despair began to thaw. We grieved, and we held onto one another. We laughed too, at memories of him. In some mysterious way life came back to us from the dead. My mother became a Christian as a result of that dream. Family members, still pre-Christian, remember the dream to this day.

The "why" question never gets answered because it's the wrong question. It's often an invalid question that makes an invalid of those who pursue it. Mostly it stems from or introduces us to victim thinking.

We are in Christ and no matter what occurs in life, we cannot look for an answer outside of our placement. The two best questions to ask are found in the account of the Day of Pentecost. "What does this mean?" (Acts 2:12) and, "What shall we do?" (2:37). As believers we must always ask questions in line with our identity. More than wanting answers, we must seek Presence. The Comforter is the only One who can help us. In His Presence I get to ask my favorite question of all, "Lord, what is it that you want to be for me now, that you couldn't be at any other time?"

That question has always been answered.

Personal Notes

What is the best question for you right now in your current situation?

Rejoice well, give thanks strongly, and ask it. If you need the Comforter, ask for Him. He will never leave you nor forsake you. In the Kingdom, mourning never goes unaccompanied. It is always linked with joy. Isaiah 61:3. The Lord is pursuing your heart. It's time to live again.

Turn weakness into a joyful vulnerability

There is a strength in weakness that only God can bring. He has a way of investing Himself into our lowest place to release an empowerment that changes a deficit into an advantage. He is so supremely confident in His own ability that he can easily afford to choose the weakest elements possible from humanity to represent Him. He is joyously accomplished in developing the kinds of people who have been written off by everyone else (1 Corinthians 1:26–29). His talent in doing everything with nothing is masterly. He turns our potential into something actual. He is never fazed or diminished by the inabilities of people but takes great delight in empowering them to be what they could not possibly become by their own efforts.

His delight in this process is so palpable that it transfers to our own hearts also. When faced with a peculiar limitation, Paul wanted God to remove it (2 Corinthians 12:7–10). This is always our prime response to anything bigger than we can handle. "Take it away from me," we pray. Of course that happens on occasion, because the Lord is our Deliverer. Sometimes He sets us free from circumstances and other times He emancipates us from within the situation. The former is a discharge from the incident itself. The latter is a desire within Him to demonstrate Who He is for us in the event we must face. We seldom mature in God's Presence by just being set free from everything. We really need to learn how to work out our salvation in awe and delight because He loves to work in us for His own good pleasure (Philippians 2:12–13).

Maturity in spiritual terms is about becoming Christlike. There is no possibility in this happening if we are unwilling to face adversity and pass our tests. Maturity is concerned with developing the same attitude and approach to life that characterized Jesus in His walk with the Father. David was a "man after God's heart" because He pursued intimacy as a way of life. Caleb was a "man of a different spirit" because he revered God's majesty and pursued it in every conflict.

All the heroes of faith in Hebrews 11:32–34 did exploits in the Kingdom because they discovered who God was for them in the circumstances they faced. They all learned how to draw strength in their moments of weakness. Heroes are people who have been sharply tested. They have trusted God when others around them ran away (2 Samuel 23:8–12). Overcoming is an attitude. Caleb had it in abundance (Numbers 13:30) when most of his fellow spies were dominated by what they had seen. Joshua and Caleb faced down the angry mob and their frightened teammates. They spoke out of their place of confidence in the majesty of God (Numbers 14:8–9), but cowards won the day. That was the moment where Israel lost its inheritance.

The stakes we are playing for are high. The tests are designed to produce men and women who can hold high office in the spiritual affairs of a nation.

We must learn how to turn our weakness into a joyful vulnerability to the sovereignty and supremacy of God. We make our weakness an offering to His Majesty. It is a joyous transaction, a delightful interaction. We can bow to His grace because its power alone can meet every need we imagine. Power is stimulated by the elated surrender of our fragility. When we are weak, then we can know strength. Maturity is the capacity to be moved from an excessive awareness of weakness to an intensified appreciation of the majesty of God.

In regard to our weaknesses, we must learn to be glad. To have a bright shining pleasure in talking with excessive pride about the superiority of Jesus. Contentment is the peaceful happiness that comes when we are in awe of how God feels about us.

Gladness, boasting and contentment in Jesus all play a vital part in the surrender of weakness to the supremacy of Jesus. Turning weakness into a joyful vulnerability to the majesty of Jesus will take us into a dimension of Kingdom life that will empower us to experience Heaven on earth in our circumstances.

Is your perception of your inabilities greater than your appreciation of majesty? How would a potential hero of faith turn that around? What are the components of developing an attitude of: "When I am weak *then* I am strong?"

When you agree with Heaven... then you release its resources

What agreements do you need to make with the Lord about your life? What provision is currently held up because you are out of alignment with your identity? Make a new confession and your proclamation will change.

When God points to a deficiency in your life, He is introducing you to your next miracle

There is no condemnation to those who are in Christ Jesus who are seeking to pursue their identity in Him. We are in Christ, learning to be Christlike. The Father loves strategic life exchange. He loves to take our bad habits and replace them with attributes of His Beloved Son.

The Holy Spirit adores the interactions with us that take us into a lifestyle of righteousness. He loves to make war on the flesh. He cherishes freedom and is absolutely delighted to make Jesus real to us, in us, and through us.

When God points out a part of our life that is not working, He is pointing to the site of our next victory. The Holy Spirit rubs His hands with glee at the thought of the blessing, freedom and release that He can bring to us in this area of our life.

God is not ashamed of us, or angry at us. He is planning brilliant things for the deficient parts of our lives. This is what Jesus died for… our freedom from sin. This is why the Holy Spirit is given to us… to make us like Christ. Because He loves freedom so much, all confrontations between the spirit and the flesh are a source of great joy to the Lord. He is our Deliverer! There is nothing He likes more than setting us free, making us clean and forming Christ within. This is the Glad Tidings of Great Joy! There is no condemnation, only the happy contemplation of a new freedom taking up residence in our hearts. When God wants us to change He always gives us a promise and a provision that is centered on the fullness of Christ.

He wants us to be as excited and enthusiastic about becoming like Jesus as He is in being formed in us. Make no mistake here. When God puts His finger on a part of our life that is not working… He is joyfully pointing at the site of our next miracle!

What is God pointing at next in your program of change? Ask for His enthusiasm to fill your heart. How will He make it a joyful experience for you?

Every problem has a provision attached to it

It is impossible to grow in faith unless you have something to overcome. Life is about how we meet problems, difficulties and adversity and the process of learning how we rise up and surmount such obstacles. An authentic life in the spirit requires both training and proving. Jesus learned obedience by the things that He experienced (Hebrews 5:8).

Every day we experience situations that form part of our development process. As the lessons take hold of us, the truth we are learning must be established in us so that we are changed into the likeness of the Lord. Truth not established is merely true. We can know what is truth conceptually, but until it has set us free, we have not *become* it in experience. We must prove that we are the truth in Christ and we can only do that by exhibiting our freedom.

Every circumstance revolves around the formation of Christ in us. He is our inheritance and we are joint heirs with Him. He is our promise and our provision, because He is all and in all. When we experience a negative, we must also encounter the positive that comes with it. Our question to the Holy Spirit is, "How is this situation going to form Christ in me?" Alternatively we can ask, "What does this mean?" (Acts 2:12) and "What shall we do?" (2:37).

What does this circumstance mean for our growth and development? How do we partner with the Holy Spirit to allow breakthrough to occur? We are encompassed in life by the promise of Christ in us, the expectation of glory. Therefore, every situation can have glory as part of the equation. We stand in the promise of God looking for the provision. We focus on the positive and never the negative. We watch, we pray and we learn how to stand, press in and receive under pressure.

The promise, not the problem, is our prime focus. We gain an awareness of the will of God. The promise allows us to relax, rejoice and respond appropriately in faith. We have a sense of purpose that we are unwilling to relinquish. Our attitude and approach is that a problem proves the existence of a provision. All we must do is explore the promise that is also present so that we know how to stand and what to confess.

The promise details the provision in front of us. As we move out, the faith that works by love stimulates us to discover what the Father's intentions toward us are. He is faithful and we are embracing that faithfulness.

Personal Notes

Acknowledge with thanksgiving that the problem has a provision. Ask the Holy Spirit for the correct promise. Be intentional in your confession and purposeful in your application. Love never fails.

A life that does not continually rejoice is not a life to feel good about

"Rejoice always, and again I say rejoice. Give thanks in everything; it's the will of God for you."

We are made for celebration. Everything in us resonates when we give thanks. We are at our happiest when we exult in someone or something. Elation is a tangible expression of being overjoyed. Gladness, jubilation and delight are visible characteristics that reveal to people a radiant happiness.

When we contemplate the Lord Jesus there is a release of passionate exuberance that connects us to God and opens us up to His reality. Celebration is a way of life. A necessity, not an option. It must be planned for, prepared for and practiced. We do not drift to the top of a mountain. We exhibit a commitment to all the training and preparation required to get there. Celebration demands preoccupation. It must dominate our attention to the exclusion of other things. It has to have a very high priority. If it has no precedence then Jesus has no preeminence and we are poorer because of it.

Personal Notes

What is standing between you and rejoicing as a lifestyle? Pay attention to rooting yourself in the delight that He has over you.

The enemy is not content to depress you — he needs you for an ally

Whenever we have a negative mindset and confession, we give the enemy permission to afflict us. Agreement is either the making or the breaking of us, depending upon who we align ourselves with in real terms. We allow ourselves to be overcome mostly by default. We are meek in our acceptance of situations and circumstances to the point where we become resigned to outcomes that should be challenged.

Overcoming a believer is not the prime goal of the enemy. Turning a Christian into an asset is the chief focus because then he has a resource into the family, church, business, ministry *et al*. The negativity, procrastination, doubt, fear, anxiety, anger, resentment, bitterness, passivity, unbelief and resignation generated gives the enemy so many tools and weapons in that confined space to create havoc. A believer that is so undermined becomes a Trojan horse; a means of internal destruction from without. How many relationships can be affected? How many dreams ruined and visions damaged?

Ten spies out of twelve brave men were so undone by the enemy that they ruined the chances of over a million people reaching the land of promise. The enemy works by penetration, demoralization and subversion. Homes, relationships, churches and the workplace are infiltrated with negativity. Breaches are caused in fellowship. We become prone to tiredness, weariness and inertia. The devil is the prince of the power of the air: he lives in the atmosphere. Penetrating the atmosphere to create an environment that he can live in is a major strategy. Check out the atmosphere around you. If it is not loving, joyful, peaceful, gracious and gentle… *you may have a problem!* We all know when we have an infestation of ants, mice, rats and cockroaches, the signs are everywhere. What is true in the natural is also true in the spirit. We must reclaim our own inner territory before we can recover the ground around us.

Demoralization occurs gradually. There is a softening up process: an attack on morale, general discouragement, feelings of powerlessness. People imagine the worst and become prone to worry, fear and a general malaise, a feeling that nothing much will change. We want escape, not recovery. Our prayer life is subdued and we feel resigned, indifferent. Positive people make us annoyed and we want to burst their bubble.

Our language and attitude ensnare other people. Misery always loves company. We are bored, tired, blaming everything and everyone else. Adrift from rejoicing, no faith connection. We are done! Now we are ripe for the enemy to use us in the subversion of others. We have been won over to a passive acceptance of our circumstances. By not contributing to the atmosphere positively, we become an unconscious resistor; a drag and a drain on the work and relationships. Subverted people challenge everything negatively. They murmur, complain and undermine. They are a critical, corrupting influence. They have allowed themselves to be unequally yoked to a negative.

Negative feelings and thoughts make us vulnerable to the enemy. Anxiety is tiring and tiresome! Sarcasm, cynicism and oppositional humor pulls everyone down. When something adverse happens, the first things we think, say and do tell us everything about our true spiritual condition.

When we allow ourselves to become negatively intended, we become like the enemy. When our mind is renewed, we destroy speculations and bring every thought captive to the obedience of Christ (2 Corinthians 10:5–6).

Where are we on the strategy of Penetration, Demoralization and Subversion? What are the signs of negative spiritual infestation around us? Are we contributing to that atmosphere or are we committed to changing it for good?

Read chapters 11–14 of Numbers to understand the process of destabilization that is used by the enemy. How will you counter that process?

11

Do not merely ignore the negative — learn how to use it!

We have a creative spirit within that knows how to take advantage of every situation and circumstance. One of God's prime development tools is teaching us how to move in the opposite spirit.

The teachings of Jesus known as The Beatitudes are a prime example of how life in the spirit needs to be lived in this world. Luke 6:22–35 teaches us the value of moving in the opposite spirit. We use what the enemy is doing to ensure new growth in the spirit and a renewal of Presence.

Bless those who persecute you, bless and do not curse (Romans 12:4). When we are reviled, we bless (1 Corinthians 4:12). The Father reserves blessing for those believers who are persecuted by their own kind. The enemy seeks Christians who will support his work of anger, judgment and criticism. He uses the flesh of the religious and worldly minded to attack the work of the Holy Spirit.

The Holy Spirit, though, loves the conflict. He is a master strategist Himself. "If you are reviled for the name of Christ you are blessed, because the Spirit of glory and of God rests on you" (1 Peter 4:14). I have been in prophetic ministry since 1974. It is simply not possible to be a prophet and live a life unpersecuted. "Blessed are you," said Jesus, "when people insult you and persecute you, and falsely say all kinds of evil against you because of Me. Rejoice and be glad, for your reward in heaven is great, for in the same way they persecuted the prophets who were before you" (Matthew 5:11–12).

Since I began in the prophetic there has been an ongoing attack on everything I am and all I do. Hate mail would be a kind description for some of the letters I receive. Many of the people who were my contemporaries in the prophetic since the 1970's have been broken and disillusioned by the continuous assault. The Holy Spirit has taught me to rejoice, be glad and jump for joy. Not as a reaction against what is happening, but as a response to the promise that is present during persecution.

Every time I am vilified, something is added to my account in heaven. "Your reward in Heaven" is not just about something being stored up for the afterlife. It also means that resources are increased that I can draw on in this time-space world. The Father rewards us for being persecuted. Maltreatment is always compensated. Persecution has an honorarium! Being hounded has a profit margin.

Sharing the sufferings of Christ is enormously rewarding (1 Peter 4:12–14). The Holy Spirit has taught me only to focus on the benefits, not the drawbacks, of persecution. I am blessed and that blessing must be as tangible as the ill treatment. If only my detractors realized the important contribution they have made to my ministry, I'm sure they would be aghast! When their opposition closed doors to my ministry, God paid me to stay home with Him. When people tried to stop my events from taking place, the Lord would tell me to put more chairs out.

However, it is in the area of personal growth in Christ where persecution has been so helpful. My level of personal revelation of Jesus has increased massively under human religious opposition. My teaching and writing is far more powerful now than ever before. Persecution pays off! It is in the area of personal encounter with the Lord that persecution has been such a blessing. "The Spirit of glory and of God rests on you."

I have felt God's kiss, His embrace and touch many times when provocation around my life has been extreme. I have received a love, joy and peace so powerful on those days that I could barely move with the weight of God's Presence resting on me.

The Holy Spirit is a genius at warfare. He is so good at using what the enemy is doing for our advantage. He takes every negative and turns it around. He shows us its opposite and then empowers us to become that in Jesus. It has become automatic for me now. I'm pretty fast at turning an insult into a blessing. Why be debilitated by a comment when you can find its opposite meaning and rejoice?

I took a question and answer session at a conference and a man approached me afterwards. In a voice dripping with contempt and his face an open sneer, he called me naïve. I grinned at him, clapped him on the shoulder and said, "Hey, thanks man, I really appreciate that!" When he looked nonplussed I informed him, "You just told me that I have a natural, unaffected simplicity. That I am artless and ingenuous. That is, I am frank, honorable and free from deception. I'm really encouraged"! The look on his face was priceless.

Personal Notes

We all have people around us who teach us grace and provide opportunities to practice the fruit of the spirit. Who are yours and what are they teaching you? Take every criticism and negative comment and find its opposite meaning. Ask the Holy Spirit to help you become that in your relationship with Him. Practice smiling more. Look for the blessing and the reward, they are always present. Enjoy the challenge. The Holy Spirit is a genius at making things fun, funny and exciting.

Is it possible to be in Christ and be powerless...

... or is that double-minded?

Such a thought is called an anomaly. It is an incongruent, aberration that is inconsistent. Have fun looking those words up.

God does not measure time; He measures growth

Time is relative to the Almighty. He sometimes operates within it, but mostly, it seems, outside of it. We, on the other hand, are often consumed by time and timings.

Some situations around our lives persist because we do not deal with them. We do not grow if we cannot change. How many of us have had the same situation occur but with different people? We can move jobs, change churches, escape to another location, even leave the country. The same issues continue because they are part of our inner landscape that needs recreating. We have the same tests *ad infinitum*.

The truth is that we cannot possibly fail any of our tests. We just get to take it again… and again, and again, and again. The Father has infinite patience because He knows that our immaturity will prevent us from reaching and experiencing the highest places in the spirit. He is OK with spending twenty years on a development that could have taken two years to complete. He will not open up the next thing until we have obeyed His commands in the place we are occupying. He does not measure time; He measures growth.

Personal Notes

What are the lessons you are learning at this time? Be honest. How many times have you had these assignments? How many more times do you want them?

Whatever God is, He is relentlessly

Love never fails, His mercies never cease. Everything about God is forever. He never changes. He is not capricious. His joy is eternal and His loving-kindness from everlasting to everlasting.

He is relentless in His grace for us. His love is so persistent. I have been the recipient of unfailing kindness for many, many years. I feel safe in His heart. I am overwhelmed by a goodness that never quits. I love His nature. I always know where I am in His love because He never changes.

When I finally got it, when I at last understood that He would be the same towards me yesterday, today and forever, it was like a huge weight came off my shoulders. I finally understood what real freedom was in Christ. It's the permission to be relentlessly loved regardless of my performance as a Christian. I cried, out of a deep sense of relief. Then I laughed and gave thanks and I've been rejoicing every since.

Personal Notes

What you think about God is the most important thought you will ever have! Read and meditate on Hebrews 13:18, Malachi 3:6, James 1:17 and Numbers 23:19. What do they say to you about the relentless beauty of God's nature?

There is a Quickening Spirit abroad in the earth

It is written: "The first man, Adam became a living soul. The last Adam (Jesus) became a Quickening Spirit" (1 Corinthians 15:45). The power of God to revitalize us is astonishing. In Christ we are learning to partner with resurrection life in all its forms. His capacity to impart spiritual life and momentum is amazing!

"Quicken" means that we are always empowered to respond to His voice immediately. He can change things in us super fast. The eyes of the Lord move to and fro throughout the earth to show Himself strong on behalf of people who belong to Him (2 Chronicles 16:9a).

Personal Notes

Ask the Lord to Quicken you in the spirit. Ask Him to revitalize a particular part of your life. Listen to what He says and get ready to run!

Stress is a choice that you make for yourself

Stress is always an inside job. We are in the process of learning how to put off our old nature and put on the new nature of Jesus.

The old nature is a product of our environment, upbringing, contact with a worldly system of values and our learned behaviors. We take on board negative experiences and traumatic occasions and treat them as though they are the truth about us for all time. The old self, until it is replaced in our experience, carries some weight in our personality. It supplies the head-noise, the background tape that runs on a loop incessantly in our thinking. All stress is already on that tape. When situations arise that are difficult for us, the button gets pressed and the old messages about ourselves get played. Stress is the result.

The new nature is a product of Heaven. It is the way that God thinks about us in Christ. He has nothing but approval for us because that's why He put us into Christ in the first place. So that we could always be accepted in the Beloved (Ephesians 1:6). The Lord has a way of thinking about us that builds us up, empowers us to grow, and causes us to be constantly renewed in the Spirit.

We need never lose heart because our outer man (old self) is being killed off, yet our inner man (our true self in Jesus) is being renewed day by day (2 Corinthians 4:16). We are practicing the joyful discipline of being renewed in the spirit of our mind (Ephesians 4:23). That means we are enabling our thinking to come from a source that is full of love for us and wants to see us grow, change and become more of who Jesus is for us. The new man hears a heart voice, not old head-noise.

We have put on a new self which is renewed in a true knowledge *according to* the image of the One who created him (Colossians 3:10). The true knowledge is that our head-noise belongs to the old man, crucified in Christ. Our new inner voice is made in the image of Jesus. We can only ever be fully transformed by the renewing of our mind (Romans 12:2).

Stress is caused by the way we see things and the platform from which we view them. When we consider ourselves dead to sin and alive to God in Christ Jesus (Romans 6:11), something must shift in our experience. The new shift can only be made by a new mindset. The mind set on the flesh is death (Romans 8:6) because it will attack anything that seeks to replace its own nature. The mind set on the Spirit is life and peace. It produces a reality of Christ within; we become alive to God and all the possibilities that He generates.

Our new nature has a voice that makes us alive to God. If we are to truly hear this inner voice of the Spirit we must differentiate it from all other voices. The voice of the inner man will sound exactly like the Holy Spirit! We know what He sounds like because scripture provides us with His voice indicators in Galatians 5:22–23. His voice is loving; joyous; peaceful; patient; full of kindness; edifying in its goodness; extremely faithful to who we are becoming; and full of a gentleness. All of which empowers us to move in self control. That is, our new nature with its new voice takes control over the old self and the stressors it provokes. It is for freedom that Christ has set us free.

A while ago I was chatting to a guy I was getting to know, when he made a startling confession. "I hate myself," he said, "I can't think anything good about myself." I asked him which self was doing the talking. He looked confused. "Well, you have two selves," I said, "the old one and the new one. Which one is doing the talking?" Only the old man would use the word hate and have no goodness. He saw it.

"What do I do about that voice?" he asked. "You ignore it," I replied. "It belongs to someone who is dead in Jesus. Instead of dealing with the old voice, you listen for the new which at least will tell you the opposite of the old!"

We don't counsel the old man; we do not deal with its behavior. That is the best way to keep it alive. Instead we reckon that we are dead to it but alive to God in the new man. We *replace* the old, we don't remodel it. The fruit of self control allows us to deny the rights of the old man and promote the disposition of the new man in Christ.

There is only one voice to hear. It is the voice of the Holy Spirit whose business it is to make you like Jesus. He talks to you in the way that the Father talks to His Son the Beloved. It's the same voice. Full of rest, loving, and with a quiet joy. It is the voice of patient kindness and gentle goodness that lifts our hearts to experience His faithfulness.

All other voices must be put in their place. That is why we have self control: so that we may know what is old and new self, and make decisions accordingly. There is something wonderful in saying "no" to the old self and "yes" to our true self in Jesus. It is deeply satisfying and powerfully renewing. The Holy Spirit will always (because the old nature is dead) focus our attention on the new man. He will always elevate the true self in Jesus. He does not deal with the old self because Jesus has already done that on the Cross. We are free to move about the Kingdom. Free to explore who we are in Jesus and discover what has been set aside for us to enjoy.

The new man would never choose stress when love, joy, peace *etc.* are all available for free. The new man would always choose a better thought, a new mindset, a renewal of perspective and a more excellent way to live. Stress is counter intuitive to the peace and rest of Jesus (Matthew 11:28–30). It's an immature response from a life that is not enjoying true fellowship as the Beloved.

═══════════ **Personal Notes** ═══════════

Which self are you listening to in your life? What is your head-noise doing to you? How would you discern the voice of God in your heart? What is He saying to you about how He sees you and feels about you?

Before we choose an action, we have already chosen a thought

Every action has a starting place. Every strong emotion has a beginning. There is a reason why the Father wants to take every thought captive to the obedience of Christ (2 Corinthians 10:5). All transformation originates in renewed thinking (Romans 12:2).

How we think about ourselves dominates our behavior (Proverbs 23:7) and sets our agenda in life towards other people. It sets the attitude in which we approach life. An attitude is simply a posture that we adopt or a position we take that expresses some thought or feeling. It becomes a habit and shows up constantly in our behavior. It is a habitual mode of thought. Attitude is much more than a description of an antagonistically insolent manner or posture.

Low self esteem is an attitude of mind that creates a sense of worthlessness in our own heart. Self importance is a conceit, rooted in our thought life that produces an arrogance and an overbearing attitude. All behavioral attitudes in between these two extremes have their roots in a thought process. Working on our thinking is a key part of being discipled and led by the Spirit. All teaching must model the right way to live in Christ.

Every day we wake up with an attitude, a mindset that either works for or against us. Differing situations provoke a behavioral response that is positive or negative. Certain people bring out particular responses that govern our behavior towards them. These attitudes are rooted in perceptions and emotions that are entrenched in a thought. The mind is the seedbed for all that we do and say. Negative thoughts are always confirmed by unenthusiastic emotions. Positive thoughts cheerfully validate everyone and everything.

Jesus has set us free to learn how to become like Him. "Let this mind (i.e., have this attitude) be in you, which was also in Christ Jesus, who although He existed in the form of God, did not regard equality with God a thing to be grasped. He emptied

Himself, taking the form of a bondservant. Being found in the likeness as a man, He humbled Himself by becoming obedient to the point of death, even death on a cross." (Philippians 2:5–8)

The thinking of Jesus shaped His personality as a man, His persona as a bondslave, His ministry towards humanity and His humility and obedience towards His Father. He took on new mindsets, attitudes and approaches to life so that He could fulfill the purpose of His Father. All these were deliberate thoughts and actions on His part. He thought it through! He changed His thinking to accommodate the life that was required of Him. He was not double-minded and therefore unstable (James 1:8) in His thinking, emotions and behavior.

The reason that we are in our current position is always our thinking. Our thinking brought us here; and it must therefore take us out and onward. If all our thinking has brought us to a place that we don't like, then surely it is time for a better thought!

Personal Notes

Think of a situation that is causing stress in your life. What is the basis of your thinking and attitude about it? What would a better thought and attitude look like to you? Try the thought out and get a sense of how it feels to you. Does it reveal Jesus or empower you in the fruit of the spirit? Practice until a change occurs.

Timing belongs to God...

preparation belongs to us

18

In this next season, how will you prepare the way of the Lord? What will you do in order to be ready for what He wants to bring into your life?

Your resources are your weapon, not your chain

There is only one way to live by faith. We simply must become preoccupied with God's Presence and focus on His Promises.

The faithfulness of the Lord in keeping His Word is the very currency of Heaven. We believe Him because He never lies; He is the Personification of the Truth. More than provision, we need the promise. Most of our provision will be contested. It will be the subject of warfare. A promise is the object that will compel us to receive.

When we take our eyes off the Lord and put them on our need, our current resources are always reduced. We never have enough in the natural. God's provision must arrive in our spirit first. We receive the promise in our heart always. It is the prime place of reception. Our head, encased in logic, will demand evidence in our circumstances. It looks at the balance sheet. Our heart needs only to be aware of Jesus. Faith works by love (Galatians 5:6), so Presence is crucial to believing. God is in us and will never leave us nor forsake us. So Presence is always present!

The inner man of the spirit, living in constant communion with God, always knows how to receive. The resources that are available to our Sonship are always embedded in the Promise of the Father. His word is 100% truth and therefore inviolate. It is far more easier to believe than doubt. If our true resource is the promise of God, then this must become a weapon in our hand. God's faithfulness to His Word and to us is also a resource and therefore a weapon. The Father loves his faithfulness to be tested (Malachi 3:8–11). "Prove me now," He says, "I can open a window of blessing that causes you to overflow." When we give to God, the devourer of our resources is always rebuked.

Our lack is never a chain that binds us, because the Promise always sets us free to receive. We can give everything we have to the Lord when we know how to abide in His Presence.

Very few people made Jesus exclaim. One of them was a widow (Luke 12:41–44). Jesus was watching how people put money into the temple treasury. All coins were metal. The thicker the metal, the deeper the sound it made when thrown into the laver. Attendants were trained to listen for the sound of certain coins being dropped into the treasury. They would then escort the giver to one of the better seats in the temple. The coins of the widow were so small and thin they barely registered as a sound. However, Jesus heard something!

He heard the sound of a poor widow giving all that she had gladly. He heard the sound of her worship in giving. It made Him rejoice and exclaim. Here was a person confident in the goodness of God. She could never out-give God because He is no man's debtor. She trusted in the faithfulness of God. It was her weapon. It was her true resource.

Personal Notes

Do you have a promise from the Father about your resources? Are you at least tithing into the Kingdom? First, settle the issue of your giving; then you are free to seek a promise from God's faithfulness.

Warriors do not look for sympathy; they look for majesty

Warriors do not need rescuing. They do not avoid tough situations. They see every circumstance as an opportunity to believe the Lord for something. They are privileged to trust, excited at the prospect of moving in faith. Every situation provides them with the opening to explore the heart of God and discover His favor. They delight in any occasion that supports their growth and learning.

They want to develop a revelation of God that is so extensive it will cover every eventuality. They welcome opportunities to advance and increase faith. Revelation of Jesus governs every area of their life. We should all know the attributes of God that are required for involvement with God at a high point of warfare.

Warriors know that opposition will be present on days and occasionally fierce and protracted. At some point we must all experience the clash between two kingdoms. Warriors are people so fascinated with Jesus that they can never be intimidated by the enemy.

There is a place in the spirit set aside for us where we make the enemy confused. We weary him by our rest. We discourage him by our faith. We demoralize him with our joy. We depress him by our endurance. Our favor is dispiriting to him; our grace defeats his objectives. Warriors are people who are not subject to the staleness of the enemy because they know how to refresh themselves.

It is so important to be confident in God. We are designed in Christ to live a life unashamed and uncondemned. Warriors make choices that arise out of their confidence in the favor and goodness of God. To be led by the Spirit means that we may constantly rejoice in the nature of God towards us. We pray joyfully out of the favor that we always possess in Christ. We look for outcomes that are in line with His sovereignty. We are never staring defeat in the face. The enemy is when he looks at us. We do not live in our circumstances, we live in Christ. Therefore, we are not subject to external pressures; only the gentle internal compulsion to give thanks.

Personal Notes

What has been set aside for you in your current situation? In your present circumstances, what is growing in you regarding the nature and attributes of God? Focus on these and rescue is not required.

Always leave a door open to possibilities

Jesus said, "All things are possible to him who believes" (Mark 9:23). The origin of the word "possible" has its roots in the concept of being made powerful, capable, strong and mighty. It is a word relating to empowerment. God gives us power by putting us into a state of favor with Him. He puts us into Christ, which is a state of grace with incredible favor attached. In this place, everything is possible, doable and attainable.

If we can conceive of something in our hearts, it can be realized in experience. Promises are the engine room of possibility. When God gives us a promise, He is releasing us from logic to imagination. He wants us to see beyond the problem to its fulfillment. A promise takes us away from Egypt and moves us towards Canaan. A promise is a guaranteed outcome that empowers us to walk the steps towards freedom and realization.

The Father loves our impossibilities. He adores the moment when He can step into our helplessness and hopelessness and make His intentions clear. A promise announces His Presence in the very circumstances that would cause unbelief in us. When life makes us disabled in the natural world, He comes from Heaven to lift us into another dimension of being.

"With people it is impossible, but not with God; for all things are possible with God" (Mark 10:27). He makes the unthinkable become imaginable. That which is beyond the bounds of possibility is now in Christ brought within reach.

A promise is more than just a powerful word. It is the intention of God made tangible. God delights in working in us so that we can conceive what is in His heart for us. We are set free from the rigid confines of rational thinking when our spirit soars into the realm of God's inclination. Our soul (mind, emotions and will) is earthbound but our spirit lives in the Presence of God. Our spirit is free to roam the place of dreaming. The Gospel restores humanity to the place of vision, design and aspiration. The Good

News of Jesus Christ removes our bondages for all time and pushes us into a kingdom where all things are possible.

"When the Lord turned again the captivity of Zion, we were like those who dream. Then our mouths were filled with laughter and our tongue with joyful shouting. Then they said among the nations, 'The Lord has done great things for them.' The Lord has done great things for us. We are glad." (Psalms 126:1–3)

The Gospel is so amazing it borders on fantasy. The Good News is so incredible it's almost too good to be true. In the world, if something sounds too good to be true, someone is being conned. In the Kingdom, if its not too good to be true, it isn't God!

On the Day of Pentecost (Acts 2) God announced His intention with an outpouring of the Spirit; which would make it possible for people to access the Kingdom through prophecy, visions and dreaming, as part of the new reality of being in Christ. Peter in his preaching that day refers back in time to a prior promise given to Joel (2:28–32).

Prophecy, vision and dreams take us into the realm of God's intention and possibility. They help us to bypass the natural mindset with its over reliance on rationale and the need to understand everything before we make a decision. Prophecy, vision and dreaming are part of the principles of faith where we learn to trust in the Lord with all our heart (inner man of the spirit) and not lean on our own understanding (Proverbs 3:5–6).

Walking by faith requires an acknowledgement that He has spoken and we are moving in obedience. He makes our path straight so that progressively we move more easily from the impossible to the possible.

In the Spirit, everything is doable. He first must move us forward in our believing. We must come to a place of agreement. Yes! God can do this! Then we take the first step necessary in our own obedience. God can do it, but the way He will do it, He may not reveal. We trust and move; He makes it possible.

God seldom reveals the process by which He will do the impossible for us. He does not want us to be distracted from Presence, Promise and Trusting. Trust in the Lord with all your heart i.e., complete focus on Him. He will do it. Its always a possibility.

Explore your own promises and prophecies from the Spirit. What do they say about Who God is for you? These words contain the power that lifts you into a different realm of possibility. Use these words to regain a stronger sense of God's Presence. Then focus on the promise and allow your heart to be empowered. When trust is high, take the first step into God's possibility for you.

People want new, but think old

Every time I take a church, organization or a business through transition, we hit this particular crisis. It is not hard to help people envision the future. It is easy to inspire people about the purposes of God. People love His promises — but not the process which is attached. Generally people wish to obtain an impartation that means they can receive without having to be changed. That is not ministry; that is magic. God does not do magic.

When God breaks through in power, we must follow through in process. The church is full of people who have been touched but not changed. The key component to being turned into another man or woman always lies in the mind. Transformation comes through the renewing of the mind (Romans 12:2).

We must be delivered from the very thing that made ministry inevitable. If we have to be set free, it follows that we must have been in bondage. The natural way of thinking is foolishness to the uninitiated (1 Corinthians 2:6–16) because they cannot be understood in logical terms. God speaks to provoke faith and we always respond in faith, trust, desire or need. We can only follow up our response by changing the very mindset that created the deficit in the first place.

If we have not changed, we have not learned. If our thinking has not been seriously adjusted then our response will diminish over time. If that happens too many times we become negatively intended; world weary, pessimistic and even cynical.

We want new, but we cling to the old way of doing things. When God breathes on a structure it inevitably comes apart. An old structure cannot bear the weight of a fresh move of God. A fresh impetus of the Spirit requires a new wineskin to accommodate and mature what God is doing.

We think that our first response is our only obligation. Going to the altar is not our response to God, it is our acknowledgement that we are in need and things must change. Our true response comes after our initial agreement with God about our condition.

We need to follow up, and open our life to an ongoing transformation. The renewal of our thinking is the key to change.

It simply is not possible to accept the new and remain in partnership with the old. Some things must change or the new will dissipate. We have all squandered too much of God's blessing without being changed for the better.

Personal Notes

What new experiences are you having at this time? What fresh encounters are you receiving? How do you plan to keep them? What fresh moves of God are you praying for? How will you prepare the way of the Lord? What is the next phase of thinking that you must accommodate? Write down the areas in your mind where renewal is required.

23

Live in harmony with God's delight

God is amazingly loving and kind and gracious. He is deeply affectionate towards His people. He has set His heart upon us and simply will not be deflected from the outpouring of His love (Deuteronomy 10:15). He sets us apart for His own possession. There is a joy, a pleasure, an enjoyment and a delight that the Lord finds in us. This is mirrored in the face of Jesus and the Presence of the Holy Spirit in our lives.

We are in the process of learning how to reciprocate the same pleasure towards Him that we receive from Him. The testimonies that we have of His affection empower us to walk with Him in a manner consistent with His Nature. When we know what God is truly like, then we are able to walk with Him in the beauty of Who He is for us. My testimony is that He is the kindest person that I have ever known. He has been relentlessly kind to me for many, many years. My heart is now settled into a routine based on His disposition towards me.

David wrote a specific song (2 Samuel 22) in the day that He was completely delivered from the hands of all his enemies. My favorite verse in this song is verse 20, "He also brought me forth into a broad place. He rescued me, because He delighted in me". His songs were always his testimony of Who God was for him (Psalms 119:24). They brought the necessary wisdom that would enable him to draw upon in other times of trouble.

We partner with God's delight. It is a vital part of our worship and our objectivity in life. It is like fitting two joints together. The measurements are precise so that the joint is both pure and strong. Handcrafted work has a harmony to it that is unbreakable. We are His workmanship, created in Christ (Ephesians 2:10) and the craftsmanship requires an excellence of execution.

Harmony involves both parties giving themselves to a divinely established relationship. There is however a hierarchy in harmony. The Lord always initiates and we always respond. He has the pre-eminence because He is always first to initiate. When the Lord gives His Word, He expects that we would receive it with great delight and hold onto that word in our heart with utmost affection (Psalms 40:8). We remain in constant agreement; like-minded with the Lord in His consistency. Harmony in delight is unity with affection.

Whenever our hearts are overwhelmed by anxieties it is God's delight in us that releases necessary and valuable comfort (Psalms 94:19). Delight begets delight. There is a high degree of pleasure in all the Lord's interactions with us. The Father is greatly pleased about Jesus. In putting us into Christ, He has joyfully made us vulnerable and susceptible to His delight. He loves us as He loves Jesus.

Delight is one of the chief expressions of His heart towards us in Christ. Whenever we see the words *gladness, joy, cheer, rejoice, glory in,* and *delight*; it is always expressive of His pleasure in us and the deep love He has for His involvement with us in the Beloved.

Life in Christ is to be fundamentally enjoyed! We relish our interaction with Jesus. We revel in the power of the Holy Spirit. We are captivated by the Lord because He has captured our hearts. Each day then brings a fresh determination to abide in His joy and delight. To allow ourselves to be touched afresh by His joy in us.

We bring that same harmony in delight into all our conflicts. Caleb was a man of a different spirit (Numbers 14:24) because he could bring harmony in delight onto the battlefield. "If the Lord is pleased with us, then He will bring us into this land and give it to us… only do not rebel against the Lord or fear this people, for they will be our prey. The Lord is with us!" (Numbers 14:8–9). He understood the value of conforming our hearts to God's essential nature.

Partnering with delight enables us to realize the dreams and desires that God has for us (Psalm 37:4). When we connect with His delight in us, we rejoice in all that He is towards us. His delight is the platform for our worship. When we have a revelation that we are His Beloved then we behave as one wonderfully loved. We act in harmony with His affection.

Finding the true place of harmony in His affection and pleasure provides us with a broad place in which to live securely in His love and to have an expectation of His favor in all circumstances.

Personal Notes

It is time to sit quietly before the Lord with no agenda other than to hear His words of pleasure over you. You are in Christ; therefore, you are worthy of love and affection. Put away low self esteem and poor self worth. They belong to the old you and therefore you are dead to them. Be alive to God's heart for you. What do you hear?

24

If we have not changed...

We have not learned

What have you heard in recent times? What has impacted your heart? What did you learn? What has changed in you? This is the process by which we are converted to His likeness. To ignore it is to stay in the place of wanting but not attaining.

Rethink your assumptions

If all our thinking has brought us to a place that we do not like, it is time to acquire some new thoughts. Our thinking always leads us somewhere. It is our responsibility to ourselves to ensure that our thinking is compatible with God's great heart towards us.

Thinking produces an acceptance, whether true or false. As a man thinks in his heart, so is he in life (Proverbs 23:7a). It is vital to check out our own self worth before the Lord. If it is good then we will live in a place of effortless rejoicing. If the giving of thanks requires much effort, it is our thinking that must be adjusted.

In grace we are all empowered to think highly of ourselves. Indeed, it is impossible to be in Christ and not think from a high place of appreciation of all that God has done and is doing. It is the launching pad for true worship. The acceptance of ourselves in the beauty of Jesus. If one of His Names is Wonderful, and we are in Him, it is appropriate to have a sense of wonder about ourselves and what God is creating in us.

We are encouraged not to think more highly of ourselves than we ought to think (Romans 12:3). This injunction makes me smile. Firstly, it is given in the context of not being conformed to the worldly way of thinking about things. Secondly, it is given in the context of a mind renewal being the basis for a radical life transformation. Thirdly, how we think is meant to prove the good, acceptable and perfect will of God. Fourthly, we are not told how high we are supposed to think of ourselves! We are told to think in a way that blends being calm with walking in faith! There is a lot of permission in that paradox. We simply must find the true place of acceptance in God's vision for us.

Thinking creates expectation. If our thought life is poor, our possibilities in life are much reduced. The assurances of God create a warmth and a trust that empower us to explore the nature of God and discover our true identity. As our identity begins to unfold, our sense of anticipation is quickened. It leads us to a new belief about ourselves and a fresh assumption that moves us into a great expectation of God.

The Holy Spirit is brilliant at moving us from theory to practice of the truth. The truth creates a fresh experience of God because it always leads us to encounter. Without experience in our relationships we cannot possibly grow beyond the initial connection. All relationships grow by encounter and experience of one another. What is true in the world is true also in the Kingdom. There are no ongoing encounters outside of the work of the Holy Spirit.

When we rethink our assumptions, it is the work of the Holy Spirit to empower our conclusions into an embrace of truth that sets us free to accept who we are in Christ, and step in to the freedom that He is creating around us. There is a new space opening up for us in the life of Christ. The next phase of our growth begins with some new thoughts about who we are now and who we are supposed to become next in Christ.

Personal Notes

How would you categorize your thinking about yourself? Poor; not great; OK; could do better; very good; outstanding? What assumptions require rethinking? Pick on the ones that are most damaging or have the least expectancy. The Holy Spirit is ready for a conversation.

We contract when we resist God; we expand when we submit

When we say yes to God we must by definition say no to something else. The reverse of that is also true. When we say no to God it is because we have already chosen something or someone else instead. Counting the cost of both decisions is therefore a viable exercise in discipleship.

When we resist the grace of God, we confine ourself to the present and must therefore redefine our future in this world and the kingdom. We constrict the freedom we can experience in the Spirit. Life takes on new limitations that cramp our capacity to enjoy who we are in Jesus. Our ability to rejoice and give thanks can often be a noticeable casualty. We are less enthusiastic about worship and expressing our gratitude and adoration of the Lord Jesus. Prayer becomes stultified. We are reduced in active faith and find simple trust to be difficult. The vibrancy of Christ within, the full expectation of glory is weakened. We shrink into a lack of expectancy.

When we respond to the voice of God, we grow. Increase is hugely important to the Father. He loves fullness and abundance. He longs to see His people moving in the full flow of their divine inheritance in Christ. A positive response will always broaden our experience and create an internal culture of permission and release.

Obedience enlarges our capacity to be trusted by the Lord. Our vision is amplified. All true development stems from obedience. Without a reverence for Lordship we cannot grow beyond a certain level. Everything remains outside of reach. The high places in God depend upon the low places being conquered.

When we say "yes" to the Lord we come into a greater sense of Who He is for us. He is not available to a casual seeker, but is wholehearted towards people of the same disposition (2 Chronicles 15:2). Agreement and alignment create a larger tendency to magnify the Lord.

Think of areas in your life where you are suffering a contraction and trace it back to your last response in that area. It's time to turn it around.

If you are in a good place but still not seeing an increase, it is time for an upgrade. Allow the Holy Spirit to provoke you into enlargement.

To increase significance, we must upgrade our focus

Sometimes life can be so busy we lose sight of what is most important. We all need to put time into the schedule for personal reflection and not allow anything to override our desire for greater significance.

Focus allows us to see the Lord in our circumstances. It sharpens our worship and maintains our thanksgiving at a level that abuses the enemy. Jesus is the center of attraction in our hearts. The time spent in real focus is amply repaid in our lives. We are able to do more in less time, often with less expenditure of resources.

Focus makes our faith more sharply defined. We become clear and distinct in our expectations of favor. Significance is increased by focus. We carry a greater sense of weight in the Spirit. We are excited by what we are magnifying in the Lord.

Personal Notes

What significance are you called to in the Spirit? What focus is required to attain that place?

Make it a rule of life that you will never talk about your own limitations and failings without, in the same breath, magnifying the Lord for His all sufficiency and greatness!

God's greatness overwhelms our inadequacies. What do you need to magnify in the Lord at this time? If, right now, you will truly worship Him (regardless of how you feel), your spirit will rise and you will see yourself differently.

The enemy cannot penetrate God's comfort

It is impossible to live on the front line and not be wounded. We cannot be a prophet and not be persecuted. Some battles leave scars. Relationships disappoint. Life brings grief and brokenness at times. We are undone by our own carnality, embarrassed by our own stupidity.

The valley is where we connect with God in the deepest level of our humanity. No pit is so deep He is not deeper still. In the lowest place of our experience the Father has released the full potency of the majestic Holy Spirit.

The role of the Comforter is the most powerful and the least understood function of the Holy Spirit. In all other roles He serves the Father and the Son. In this role He is uniquely Himself.

He is the Spirit of consolation. He is full of grace, kindness and mercy. He can rejoice with those who rejoice and weep with those who weep. He is the most patient, tender, gentle and loving person when we are in the place of grief and despair. He comforts us in all of our distress. In the trouble that is self inflicted He brings encouragement, forgiveness and cleansing. When desolation is caused by the actions of another He supports us into a place of favor and ensures our heart is not ravaged by bitterness.

Some situations are mercifully short but we still need His Presence so that our recovery is not held up by rejection. Other situations may last several years or longer. This is likely to be a part of our development through brokenness. We must come to the end of ourselves in order to be radically changed. The Comforter holds us in His hands and heart to sustain us on that journey.

People don't want comfort. They prefer a quick fix. There are circumstances and times when the power of God is bent against us. He loves us too much to leave us unbroken, but He will always give us a Comforter. We need the succor and support of the Spirit. We must ask for Him! Only He can alleviate our sufferings and assuage our guilt and condemnation. Only He can make our lives glad. He reassures us, brings refreshing and creates a peacefulness within that empowers us to kneel and kiss the hand that hurts.

Jesus learned obedience by the things that He suffered (Hebrews 5:8), and so must we if we are to be trusted with greater things. It is also the role of the Comforter to tell us when grief and mourning are over, so that we can return to joy.

The enemy has power over us in the low places if we do not experience the fullness of the Spirit in consolation. We become prone to disillusion, rejection, resentment, anger, bitterness and depression. The Comforter is our shield against the depredations of the enemy who would take advantage of our downfall.

In comfort the Holy Spirit upgrades our own lovingkindness, patience and humility. We learn afresh how radically we are loved. The role of the Comforter is to ensure that we are as beautifully, radically loved in our demise as we are when we are doing well. God never changes. He is always consistently the same. The Comforter is the Presence of God in the worst possible place in our lives.

Personal Notes

Ask the Lord for the Comforter. If your life has too many negative outlooks, you need encouragement. Just ask, the answer will be yes! (2 Corinthians 1:20)

The greater the discomfort, the closer you are to giving birth

Nothing that is worth having is ever obtained cheaply. To birth the dream that is in your heart will be painful. It will cost you in time, effort, sweat, money and distress. You cannot hand over the bad bits for others to do. There are no bailouts if you are the one who is creating something. If you want something badly enough you must go through the pain of getting it. Otherwise, your non-sacrifice is also a sign of your lack of passion.

Part of us must be indelibly printed in what is coming forth. Joy must be present in the incubation process or we will not go full term in what God is doing in us. When I started Brilliant Book House I had no idea it would be painful, tiring, all consuming, fretful, annoying and burdensome. It has been all those, as well as joyful, exciting, scary, brilliant, fun, rewarding and outrageously creative. I love it!!

Every time we have gone through something painful, something new happens. The creative process contains joy and pain. We are learning that the downside creates the upside. We are partnering with God better in the process. We are much improved in our style of taking risks. We actually have style now!

We have won through into a really good place in recent times. Now we are taking a scarily good risk. A huge jump in our own growth and development. I may be writing this segment just for me. I can feel the pressure growing; I expect to experience the excitement building and the faith growing. Enlargement here we come!

30

Personal Notes

What happened to your dream? If you set it aside, pick it up. If you are experiencing the discomfort, what else is present? Take a fresh grip of the Holy Spirit and ask the questions you need to ask. Get back on the roller coaster and enjoy the journey.

What does God want to be for you now?

In any circumstance, the two best questions that we can ask are: "What does this mean?" and "What shall we do?" They were both asked at Pentecost (Acts 2:12, 37), when people were faced with events that were way beyond the norm.

The first question always relates to relationship. What does this mean for us? How will this affect our fellowship? Everything that God does is relational — *everything*. There is therefore a relational basis to everything that God allows into our life. Our first response then must be to inquire of the Lord concerning how our relationship must develop next. This is crucial for us, absolutely vital. If faith works by love (Galatians 5:6) then it works best and easiest in the context of relationship. What we do at the beginning of any new situation is vital to the outcome.

The enemy would like us to connect with the difficulty first. That way it is easier for him to deny us the outcome that he does not want us to enjoy. If we focus on the event, we become susceptible to a series of unhelpful thoughts and emotions that at this point may not be connected to the fruit of the Spirit. It is the Nature of God that guarantees Presence and produces the love, joy and peace that makes moving in faith much more simple.

"What does this mean for our relationship Lord" is a fabulous question at the start of something. We know that He loves to initiate everything, so this question easily translates into the thought: "He has plans to upgrade our relationship and fellowship and will use this situation to achieve that purpose."

Now, at the very least, we are madly curious or really excited. Any negative impact from the situation is denied an effect as we contemplate God's heart toward us. We rejoice, give thanks and move into the prayers that God loves to answer. "Lord, what is it that you want to be for me now? How do you want to use this situation? What do I do to support your purpose?"

"What shall we do" opens us up to a great response to divine purpose. How do we position ourselves, what is our primary focus and what is the correct mindset? These are great supplementary questions that allow us to ensure that our thinking is moving in the same purpose as the Lord's. If our first response is to engage with the circumstance then the outcome begins to fade.

When we focus on relationship both Presence and purpose are highlighted and we are empowered by the outcome. We see the end from the beginning and our hearts become fixed. When we focus on the situation first, the problems overwhelm our vision and our emotions contend against right thinking. We become unstable, tossed around like the surf of the sea (James 1:6–7). It is harder to receive anything positive from this place of unrest.

If we have been taken out of fellowship by events, there is only one thing to do that will guarantee a brilliant recovery: we must repent wholeheartedly. Repentance takes all the work of the enemy and sets it to zero effect. Repentance restores us to the wonderful experience of grace.

Grace is the empowering Presence of God that gives us all the confidence we need to come before God, recharged in His love. Grace both restores us to Presence and Purpose and also maintains the passion in our hearts to work with the Lord.

God loves us too much to leave us where we are (Jeremiah 29:11).

Personal Notes

The present situation is about relationship first. So, go ahead, ask the question and record your answer.

God allows us our preferences, but not our prejudice

I prefer rugby to American football because it's a faster, tougher, more action packed and compelling spectacle to watch. The game is based on momentum and movement and seldom stops. I was so bored, I became prejudiced against football. For love of my American friends I persevered watching football, and have grown to enjoy the game and be excited by it.

Rugby is forty minutes of mayhem followed by a tea break, and then forty minutes of mayhem. It is an eighty minute game that takes eight minutes. It was so hard for me to get into the stop/start nature of American football. That and the fact that a guy on the side who has nothing to do with the teams can throw a flag on the field and the game cuts to a commercial where I am forced to listen to ads for products I have no intention of buying! Americans are brought up on this stuff and have developed coping mechanisms to alleviate the aggravation. As an Englishman watching a sport spectacle, the idea that a commercial could interrupt play still horrifies me, but I have learned to switch off and switch on. The only commercials I enjoy in football are the Super Bowl ones, where at least we are turning a crisis into a comedy. At the time of writing I am loving the playoffs and looking forward to the Bowl. I love College ball also — it's a hoot!

Prejudice overwhelms us and prevents us from seeing and experiencing so many things in life. A prejudice, once formed, can take a long time to undo. It can kill our enjoyment of so many things. Having a preference for one thing over another is cool. Turning that preference into a prejudice against someone or something is extremely damaging for us, and probably the other person.

How much divisiveness do we allow around our lives because we have moved too easily from a preference to a prejudice? A prejudice is our own responsibility. No one makes us prejudiced. The actions of others should have no bearing upon our response. We do the right thing regardless of people and circumstances; because we want to live the right way before God.

As children, we can be born into prejudice and we unconsciously take on the attitudes of the older generation around us. When we come to Christ, He will do violence to anything that limits our capacity to receive and walk with Him in love. Prejudice makes prisoners of us all. It binds our hearts and limits our capacity to walk in fullness.

Prejudice is a demonic device because it is uniquely designed to kill both sides. The object and the subject both die. For the enemy it is a "heads you lose, tails I win" situation. Prejudice makes losers of us all.

The starting place for undoing a prejudice is our own repentance. I love repentance so much! It takes all that the enemy has done and turns it to zero in our hearts. Repentance is the key to unlock what has already bound our hearts. Wholehearted repentance is the foundation for a change of thinking. A mindset can only be replaced by another mindset. "A mind set on the flesh is death, but the mind set on the Spirit is life and peace." (Romans 8:6)

Repentance restores us to God, creates the possibility of new thinking and leads to a new perspective that empowers a different approach. We must take responsibility not only for what we have done wrong, but also for the lack of blessing that we could have released had we not been bigoted or biased.

Walking in love with Jesus means that we have His permission and blessing to overflow in grace and favor to all that we meet in the course of life. Prejudice prevents blessing from flowing, and we are the poorer because of it.

Personal Notes

Look at the relationships around your life. How many have been damaged by a perception or a thought rooted in a bias? How much and what manner of blessing has been restricted through you because of partiality? How much of your heart has been closed off or shut down due to your own intolerance?

Take the steps of recovery that repentance offers to you.

There is no frustration in Heaven

Whatever has been bound already in Heaven is capable of being bound on earth. Whatever has been loosed in Heaven can be released into the earth (Matthew 18:18). This is one of the major keys of the Kingdom (Matthew 16:19). If frustration does not exist in Heaven, there is no need to give it life through our circumstances.

It is a worldly concept. It is a negative confession that we have been stymied, obstructed and invalidated in our forward movement. We have allowed people, situations and the enemy to impede our progress. Frustration opens a door to negativity and makes our emotions vulnerable to disappointment and disillusion. Pessimism is our reward.

In the Spirit, we are learning how to turn a negative to our own advantage. The antidote to frustration is patience, peace and joy. Why focus on the vexation? A negative proves the existence of a positive because all of life is a paradox. A paradox is two apparently conflicting ideas contained in the same truth. We have to be last to be first and give to receive! A paradox contains opposites. Frustration therefore has a Heavenly counterpart.

Frustration is a sign to us that an upgrade is waiting for us. An available increase needs to be picked up. Another possibility is present. Frustration is also a sign that we are not being creative enough in Jesus. There are better questions to ask and superior viewpoint to be attained. Heaven is never diminished, and neither are we in Christ. God always causes us to triumph in Christ (2 Corinthians 2:14). Frustration is a big, wonderful indicator that something excellent is also present. God works all things together for good. Frustration will always turn to celebration if used properly.

N.B. See the interactive journal "Manifesting Your Spirit" for a longer article on frustration.

Personal Notes

Use your frustration wisely. What needs to be loosed in you and your circumstances? The Holy Spirit seeks to release a positive from this negative. What is your part in this partnership?

He talks to us by pointing at Himself

The Lord has only one source for communication to us. It is the life of Jesus within. Your old self is dead; your real self is Christ. When Jesus points to Himself, we get the message.

So when He talks about Himself, He is also talking about who we are. Who are you in Christ?

The Fruit of the Spirit
is a more potent weapon
against the enemy than the gifts

We must defeat the enemy personally and then we have power over the enemy in ministry. We cannot take ground from the enemy if he has ground in us. In warfare the enemy uses our own flesh against us. It makes sense therefore that our first line of defense is the nature of God in the fruit of the Spirit.

There is a place in the Spirit set aside for us where He manifests the character of Jesus and releases His own personality into our hearts. It is our willingness to partner with the Holy Spirit that makes the enemy so desperate. The Holy Spirit has never lost a battle to him.

When we move in love, the enemy is overcome. We weary him by our rest. We discourage him by our faith. Our patience is frustrating to him. We intimidate him with our intimacy in Christ. We demoralize him with our joy. Our peace checkmates his anxiety. We depress him by our endurance. Kindness makes him despondent. Mercy triumphs over judgment; he is dispirited by our favor. We defeat him by our grace. Goodness overwhelms hate. Faithfulness overthrows treachery. Gentleness conquers the harshness of his heart. Our self control thwarts his every purpose. We win by staying fresh, longer.

Our inner Presence produces power over the enemy. What will you allow in the Spirit to dictate your situations? How will you develop and use the attributes of God in your pursuit of overcoming the enemy?

It takes God to love God

Nothing that we give to God can originate within us. We can only love God because we ourselves are loved first by Him (1 John 4:19). Everything that we have is given to us first by God (James 1:17). The way we come into salvation is the way that our fellowship with God is generated. He initiates and we respond. It will always be this way.

"A man can receive nothing unless it has been given to him from Heaven" said John the Baptist. Paul had a similar revelation to John and the other two apostles when he wrote: "Who has first given to Him that it may be paid back to him again? For from Him and through Him, and to Him, are all things." (Romans 11:35–36)

Everything comes from Heaven to the Christ in us, and then comes through Him and is returned back to God via worship, prayer and acts of service by the Holy Spirit. All fellowship with God is derived from a relational circle that receives from Heaven and then returns it to Heaven.

Whatever the Father wants from us He always gives to us. In the New Testament, because we are in Christ, every command is also now a promise. When God commands holiness He intends to bestow the same upon us (1 Peter 1:15–16). The Holy Spirit is called the spirit of promise who seals us in Christ (Ephesians 1:13) and works within to present us as holy and blameless and beyond reproach (Colossians 1:22).

The love that we give to God was first given to us. It takes God to love God. He loves to give to us and loves to receive from us. It is in His DNA. When we had young children, we would give them money to buy us a present on our birthday. It's in our DNA too!

Ask God to love you. Ask Him for tangible expressions of His love. I have discovered Him to be very tactile. Love is not a theory but a tangible reality. We feel it, experience it in our emotions and as a physical sensation. We are moved by love. God's love is no different in its expression or its reception.

For us to love God well we must become the well Beloved.

Personal Notes

Where you are right now, ask God to pour His love upon you. Ask and keep on asking, because it's a good prayer that is in line with God's will.

Take responsibility for your blessing

The chief role of ministry is to release people to find and discover God's heart for themselves as individuals. We are not here to tell them what to do but to empower them to be sensitive to the Lord. We teach people how to walk in relationship and fellowship with the Godhead.

This means that the responsibility for their life and walk is firmly in their own hands and heart. Nowhere is this more true than in the issue of blessing. The blessings of God are our birthright in Christ. They are our inheritance. It is impossible to be in Christ and not be blessed.

People must be answerable for their own blessing. We all have a growing dependability upon God which is vital for our relationship. We must learn to take authority over everything that would prevent God's blessing from being experienced. It is vital that our lives are blessed, not optional. We need to come to the place where we are not dependent upon someone else's ministry to create a breakthrough.

We know how to receive blessing, how to maintain ourselves in blessing, and how to be a blessing to others. Taking responsibility for our own blessing is one of the principal signs of maturity.

Personal Notes

There are unclaimed upgrades stacked up over our lives. It is time to ask the Lord for specific blessing that will upgrade our lives into the place of His choosing.

37

Never underestimate
the power of God's
passion for you. Live life
in a way that prepares
you for God moments

38

Ask the Lord for a revelation and an encounter with His passion. Take a few days to seek, to fast, and to pray that your life will be filled with a new zeal for His Presence.

You won't regret it, and neither will anyone who knows you.

Align with the Father's most recent perception of you

"I see you sitting at your desk writing", said the ten year-old girl. "And the Lord came up behind you and poured a jug of really nice smelling oil all over your head. He was smiling over you. The oil soaked your hair and your clothes. You started to write and couldn't stop. You were listening and writing, listening and writing. Books, lots of books." I was at a conference on the west coast. Belinda had come to thank me for a CD of mine given to her brother in prison that led him to the Lord and turned his life around. In her words she had got her brother back, only better. She offered to pray for me and I gladly accepted.

"What do you think the picture means?" I asked her. "I think it means that all your next books are going to be written in a different way and they will have more power," she smiled before leaving with her mom.

It stayed with me for weeks. She could not know that I had been struck down with a brain virus months before and that I was struggling with my concentration and focus. I was actually afraid of getting behind my desk to write my next book. When I came to start writing, I prayed the previous day around what Belinda had seen.

The next day I felt apprehensive but also a little excited. I wrote for six hours, using my notes but also listening. It had never been easier to write. In the evening I spent time in celebration and reflection. I decided that I would align with that perception of listening and writing. I still do the research because I love the learning. However, I meditate more. My writing has a new rhythm.

Surprisingly in my everyday life I still find it hard to concentrate and I forget things: but when I sit at my desk to write, I am a different person. I have always believed that alignment is important, but this was different. I deliberately entered into a prophetic agreement and adjusted my normal methodology. After a week something evolved in my spirit. I wrote things that I had never read, heard or taught. I had to study and research what I had written like a good Berean. (Acts 17:11)

Aligning with God's most recent perception means that our prior vision of ourselves must be upgraded. We must find some new thinking, language and behavior that reflects the space we are moving into. It may take some time to make the adjustment or we may be astonished at how quickly we settle into the new place.

Personal Notes

Its time to check on any dreams, visions, scriptures and prophetic words that we have received. Do any resonate with you? If your heart is being stirred you may be looking at an upgrade and a new alignment. Ask the Holy Spirit for wisdom. Write down your thoughts and meditate on them. This is probably your moment to make a big change.

Your starting point always guarantees your outcome

Of Him are you, in Christ Jesus (1 Corinthians 1:30). The Father commands us to think afresh about our beginnings in this spiritual journey and to live from that new beginning always.

The old nature is dead and we are to consider it so for the rest of our lives (Romans 6:11). We are now engaged in practicing a life that is only alive to God and focused on our truest identity in Jesus.

Jesus is to become our all in all. We are now raised up with Him so that we may continue seeking a perspective and a lifestyle that comes from another dimension. Our thinking is set from this place. We have a new persona and a very different stature. (Colossians 3:1–3)

We always move and live from the place of Christ within (Acts 17:28). We fight *from* victory, not *towards* it (2 Corinthians 2:14), so that victory is guaranteed (1 Corinthians 15:57). Where we start from is vital. We are already in Christ by an act of God. We are learning how to stay, dwell and remain in that place.

As we learn to face every issue from the place of indwelling Presence, our perceptions undergo a radical transformation. Christ in us, the hope of glory; the confident expectation of something excellent occurring.

The old man is dead; we are a new creation in Christ. That is our starting point. We don't need counseling for our old man so much as we need schooling on our real identity in Christ. We never start life in God with a deficit. The Cross and Baptism in water give us a defined end to the life that doesn't work. Now we have a new life and each day we refresh ourselves in newness of life (Romans 6:4) and serve in newness of spirit (Romans 7:6).

When we face an issue in Christ, we learn how to see the end from the beginning. The outcome beckons us forward. "Thanks be to God, who always leads us in triumph in Christ." We are never staring defeat in the face; the enemy is constantly.

Personal Notes

Reflect on your true place in Christ. Read Romans chapter 6.

Your starting place is the indwelling Christ. As we practice newness each day, it becomes our richest experience. Living one day at a time and rejoicing in Christ within.

God is not dealing with our sin — He is establishing our righteousness

The Father loves to give us permission to be like Him — to view ourselves as He does and then to take on that identity. He gave Jesus both as Savior, to bring closure to the old nature, and as Redeemer, to turn a sin habit into righteous behavior. He gave the Holy Spirit to each of us to empower us in the process of being made in His image.

He gave us authority and the right to confess our new identity, refuse temptation, and choose righteousness. The Lord behaves towards us as though we are dead to sin and alive to Him (Romans 6:11), and gives us the authority and permission to do the same. We behave towards Him as He behaves towards us. He considers us to be dead and that our new life is hidden with Christ in Him (Colossians 3:3). Death is an end of something. He who has died is freed from sin. (Romans 6:7)

The Good News is now that we are in Christ, we get to become everything that He is in His relationship before God. "For the death that He died, He died to sin once and for all; but the life that He lives, He lives to God. Even so (in the same way) consider yourselves to be dead to sin, but alive to God in Christ Jesus," (Romans 6:10–11). As He is so are we in this world (1 John 4:17).

God has dealt with sin once and for all in Christ. He is now focused entirely on righteousness.

In Christ it is grace that reigns in life through righteousness (Romans 5:21). Jesus did not just take our sin; He became the embodiment of it, so that we could become the embodiment of righteousness (2 Corinthians 5:21). Now that we are free from sin we can become servants of righteousness. Everyday we get to present ourselves as righteous servants (Romans 6:18–19).

In the Gospel it is the righteousness of God that is always being revealed; because the righteous live by faith (Romans 1:16–17). We are learning to love righteousness. We are focused only on being right with God and enjoying all the benefits of sanctification (Romans 6:22).

This incomparable gift of being in Christ is only by God's doing. Jesus now becomes our wisdom, righteousness, sanctification and redemption (1 Corinthians 1:30).

God dealt with sin once and for all by killing Jesus. It would be an insult to Jesus if the Father still considered sin to be alive in us. Our old nature is dead; it is our new nature only that occupies His attention. The Holy Spirit works to establish righteousness as a lifestyle. He does that by empowering us to become Christlike. He reminds us always of who we are in the Beloved. He speaks to our new position in Christ. We have been raised up. We have a new disposition and a new dimension of life to focus from (Colossians 3:1–3), because our life is hid with Christ in God.

When the Spirit puts His finger on a part of our life that is not working, it is to point to our righteousness and to establish it in this part of our life. We no longer have a sin *nature*; it died. We have a sin *habit* that is being reformed into righteousness. His approach is not "get rid of this and you can become that;" rather, He says, "You are this you have no need of that."

We do not become a new person by changing our behavior; we discover the person we already are in Christ and behave accordingly. The role of the Holy Spirit is to empower that discovery and transformation.

Personal Notes

Focus on the new nature in Christ. Who does the Spirit say you are in Jesus? Write these things down and know that the Holy Spirit will joyfully establish these truths in your behaviors.

There is no internal struggle over sin; only a simple resting in the righteousness of Christ

When I speak on the truth that we are to focus only on righteousness rather than sin, the question I am asked most always concerns Romans 7:14–25:

> For we know that the law is spiritual, but I am carnal, sold under sin. For what I am doing, I do not understand. For what I will to do, that I do not practice; but what I hate, that I do. If, then, I do what I will not to do, I agree with the law that it is good. But now, it is no longer I who do it, but sin that dwells in me. For I know that in me (that is, in my flesh) nothing good dwells; for to will is present with me, but how to perform what is good I do not find. For the good that I will to do, I do not do; but the evil I will not to do, that I practice.

> Now if I do what I will not to do, it is no longer I who do it, but sin that dwells in me. I find then a law, that evil is present with me, the one who wills to do. For I delight in the law of God according to the inward man. But I see another law in my members, warring against the law of my mind, and bringing me into captivity to the law of sin which is in my members. o wretched man that I am! Who will deliver me from this body of death? I thank God — through Jesus Christ our Lord! So then, with the mind I myself serve the law of God, but with the flesh the law of sin.

In this letter to the Romans, Paul is writing to two very different groups: the Jews, who have a long and established history with God and the Law, and the Gentiles, who have no history at all. These are two groups who are coming at redemption from opposite sides. One from paganism and the other with a well formed religious tradition. Romans 7 is where this problem gets serious attention.

The Jews came from a life lived under the law as the original people of God, but who are now needing to abandon the Old Covenant to establish a New Covenant based on a different sacrifice for sin: the Messiah, Jesus.

The Gentiles, with no prior exposure to God, are coming out of gross darkness into the light. They have no concept of God and no part in Israel's religious struggle.

At some point in his letter Paul has to separate these two groups so that he can answer the very specific problem of the Jewish people, which is: "What about the law of God, given to Moses?"

Romans 7:1 is where that separation occurs. "Or do you not know, brethren (for I am speaking to those who know the law)…" In Romans chapters 6 and 8 he writes to both groups. In Romans 7 he is writing only to the Jews. Romans 7 is not for Gentile Christians in Christ. It is answering specific questions for those under law.

If this is for all believers then it clashes with the theology of life in Christ:

1. Romans 7:18 "…the willing is present but the doing is not," is in confrontation with "I can do all things through Christ who strengthens me." (Philippians 4:13)

2. Romans 7:19 "…the good that I want to do, I cannot," is in opposition to "God works in us to will and to do." (Philippians 2:13)

3. Romans 7:21 "…evil is present with me," opposes the truth that "I have been crucified with Christ, and it is no longer I who live but Christ lives in me and the life I now live in the flesh I live by faith in the Son of God who loved me and gave Himself up for me." (Galatians 2:20)

4. Romans 7:23 "I see a different law in my members, waging war against the law of my mind and making me a prisoner of the law of sin which is in my members," conflicts with the theology of the Cross, which states: "He that is dead is free from sin… so consider yourself dead to sin but alive to God." (Romans 6:7, 11)

A dead person has no struggle — they are laid to rest. The Christian Life begins with resting in all the accomplishments of Christ. It is continued in the same way, day after day. We begin each day with rest, rejoicing and a confession of who we are in

Christ. "I am a new creation in Christ, the old things are passed away, behold new things are coming and all these things are from God." (2 Corinthians 5:17, 18a)

Personal Notes

Practice your rejoicing in Romans 6:7–11. Develop your own confession. You are not struggling with sin; you are developing righteousness.

We can only be challenged by Goodness

It was the relationship between the Lord and Moses that first gave us the glimpse of power, significance and importance of goodness in the Kingdom. His request to see God's glory propelled Him into an encounter with goodness that opened him up to all the claims of God about Who He essentially is in Himself (Exodus 33:18–34:8). The Glory of God is that He is unending Goodness. His goodness must cover the earth in the same way that Heaven is filled with good. God's goodness was so powerful that Moses had to be placed in the space between two rocks and then covered by God's hand to protect him from the heat, the power and the passion of good.

When God walked in front of Moses and proclaimed Himself, the attributes He used are all a part of His Goodness. Compassionate, gracious, slow to anger, abounding in lovingkindness and truth, keeper of lovingkindness, one who forgives, righteous judge against the truly wicked (i.e., people of iniquity, transgression and sin).

Goodness follows us all the days of our lives (Psalm 23:6). It is the antidote to despair (Psalm 27:13) and the nature of God that most leads us to repentance (Romans 2:4). He stores His goodness up for each of His beloved children who revere Him (Psalms 31:9). Jesus went about doing good and healing all who were oppressed by the devil (Acts 10:38). The power of God's goodness was so legendary that all the nations would revere it and worship Him and the enemy would tremble because of it (Jeremiah 33:9).

Goodness has always featured in everything that God is and does. It is one of the fruits of the Spirit (Galatians 5:22) and is the fruit of Light in our lives (Ephesians 5:9).

The Goodness of God is the hallmark of every true disciple. A good man reveals his treasure of goodness to the world (Matthew

12:35) and walks in a manner worthy of God's nature because goodness pleases God (Colossians 1:10).

Goodness is critical in times of opposition and warfare. We are to love our enemies and do good to them (Luke 6:27–35). We never suspend the power to do good in any circumstance of life. Goodness has extraordinary power for the giver as well as the recipient. We overcome evil with good because it is the source of true power (Romans 12:1).

True disciples prove what is good (Romans 12:2) because they see goodness as the only lifestyle that can truly represent God. They have chosen to abound in goodness. To overflow, flourish, be extravagant, lavish and profuse. This is what makes us Christlike. All love, gentleness, grace and mercy, patience and kindness are acts that are rooted in the goodness of God. We are careful to maintain acts of goodness throughout our life. God does not give us options here. He commands goodness as a viable Kingdom lifestyle.

Indeed, every situation and circumstance is to be used to express the goodness of God. Therefore, everything that happens is a challenge to the Father of His goodness in us and through us. We are not therefore being challenged by life; oppositional people, circumstances and the enemy. We are only ever challenged by God's Goodness.

We are challenged to live, think, speak and act for the good in every circumstance. The challenge is for us to be so filled up with the goodness of God that our lives would be as radiant as Moses' face! We are encouraged by the Lord to be prepared for every good work (2 Timothy 2:21) and be equipped to do good constantly (3:17), ready for any good deed that is possible (Titus 3:1) and an example, a pattern for goodness in the earth (2:7).

True disciples represent the fullness of God's nature. They are not worldly people. They do not repay evil with evil but they always seek after that which is good for one another and for all people (1 Thessalonians 5:15). Seeking after everyone's good is the real challenge of our spirituality. He puts so many things into a true Godly perspective. To have a reputation for doing good (1

Timothy 5:10) and to be so rich in goodness that it would be our prime passion to be generous and share not only Who God is but what He has given (6:18).

No one is safe from the power of goodness. People will repent when they taste the goodness of God. Will we be taken for granted? Almost certainly. Will our goodness be abused? Count on it. Will people think we are foolish? Definitely. Here's the real truth behind all of that imposition: "Who is there to harm you if you prove zealous for what is good?" (1 Peter 3:13)

The truth is that it doesn't matter if we are maligned. We are not doing it for man's approval, but for God's glory. We are being challenged to look at life through the lens of God's goodness. To see everything and everyone in the light of God's great heart. We are God's visual aid to the earth. Through our lives, people get to taste and see that the Lord is good. We are the physical, tangible evidence that God is brilliantly, incredibly, astonishingly full of goodness. God is good. There is no higher truth.

It is time for a fresh revelation of goodness. It is time for an encounter with goodness. It is time to change our lifestyle to an ongoing experience of goodness. Ask the Holy Spirit for a radiant expression of goodness to connect with your heart.

Make a list of people around your life who need the goodness of God. Be the first to move in God's goodness. In every situation, realize there is only one challenge facing you. It is the challenge of goodness to overcome everything and release the glory of God in to the earth.

If it matters to you, then it matters to God.

Personal Notes

God is not reluctant to bless you. Quite the opposite, in fact. You are His Beloved child. Step into the place of favor and ask Him for what you need.

A renewed mind is one that will not contemplate a single day without favor

When the Father puts us into Christ, He envisages the same relationship with us that He enjoys with Jesus. We are in Christ so that all the favor He enjoys now comes to us also.

We are not given favor because of who we are, but because of who Jesus is. His favor is ours because we too are heirs of God and joint heirs with Christ (Romans 8:17). We are not given favor because of our performance as believers but because of our placement in the Lord Jesus.

Favor is a special preference of one to another. It is an advantage given from the greater to the lesser. Favor is an intentional bias. It means to consider someone as your favorite. Favor allows us to be esteemed, approved and highly loved by the Father. Everything that the Father has given to Jesus now automatically becomes part of our relationship also. Favor is a relationship. It is the currency that provides all we need in our fellowship with God. It is a lifestyle of walking with God in Christ.

As disciples we understand that favor is our highest position in Christ. It is favor that empowers us to step out of need into provision with absolute confidence that God will provide. Favor is assurance of God's heart towards us. Favor is the strongest part of our fellowship. It is the evidence in Christ that we are powerful in how we face life and circumstances. Favor makes us alive to God and active in faith. It makes us defiant against the enemy and assertive in our circumstances. Favor makes us receptive to change and available for any upgrades and increases. In favor we become energetic about who we are in Christ. Favor empowers us to be joyfully confident and expectant on life's journey.

We are never without favor; it is the means by which we cultivate intimacy and become bold in prayer. Every day carries a fresh experience of favor. A true disciple is never without it.

N.B. For the complete training in favor, visit www.brilliantbookhouse.com and look at the Favor Series.

Personal Notes

This is your time to be called up to a deeper place of relationship in Christ. In Him everything is yes and amen. You must practice favor until it is established. Where would you start? Choose one area of your life and use it as your training ground.

Christians do not lie;
they delete, distort, and generalize

We have all known people who are economical with the truth. In times of tension and relational difficulty people are fearful of the truth. We do not like our failings coming under scrutiny. We have an aversion to our words being examined. In the church, religious people try to present their words in a way that puts people off the scent. We use christianese; so-called spiritual jargon and scripture verses to back ourselves up. Often we confuse people enough that they back off and leave us alone.

In many counseling and discipling situations when I have been trying to unravel a particular situation, people feel threatened. They feel backed into a corner and come out swinging. One guy screamed at me in accusation: "You're calling me a liar; I don't believe it." I remember smiling at him and replying calmly: "I think mostly you are deleting, distorting and generalizing." His face returned to its normal color. "What do you mean?" he asked suspiciously.

As a rule, people delete what they said or did that was wrong. They distort what others said and did. They generalize about their involvement in what needs to happen next. Deletions, distortions and generalizations can be vague or specific. They are our versions of what is true. It's useful to separate out what is true from what is truth. Jesus is the truth, everything else is true or false. If something is the truth then Jesus would be visible and our spirit will witness His Presence. At some point a particular spirit will manifest itself. Truth will out.

There is no substitute for honest insight into ourselves. It is the beginning of integrity. In your current tensions and relational difficulties, are you deleting, distorting and generalizing? That ground needs to be recovered. It is a major part of your growth.

The internal power of our identity will always discover and employ the external power in a crisis

When we know who we are in Jesus, we receive the confidence necessary to pursue that identity. What the Lord says about us is a major clue to our inheritance. When we have received scripture from the Spirit that pertains to a particular calling, then all our resources will flow through that identity.

Many years ago the Lord gave me the story of Caleb (Numbers chapters 13 & 14 and Joshua 14) to read. I had little idea of how life would change. His identity was that he was a "man of a different spirit." He never backed down from a fight and had a strong revelation of God's majesty and favor. He relished the battle. In his 85th year, he reminded Joshua of a promise given to him forty years earlier by Moses. Caleb was claiming the last stronghold of the giants for his inheritance. "Give me this mountain, (Joshua 14:12) giants live here, and I will drive them out."

At some point in my deliberations, the Lord spoke to me and called me Caleb, a warrior. In the next few years several dozen people gave me the same word, though I had shared the original reference with no one. It has made a huge difference to how I approach life, obstacles and warfare.

Our identity sets us up for the life that God has envisaged. Our identity forms the agreement and the alignment that we have with the Lord. All of our resources flow to the identity that we uphold in our own hearts. Confession and proclamation rise up within us. Identity is where we stand tall in God's sight. We live in a defined way in His Presence. We know what to expect of ourselves. We accept the role that He thrusts upon us and we grow into its dimensions.

When faced with the impossible, our identity must rise up and become its true height. Who we are in Christ should always be larger in life than any issue we face. When David faced Goliath, he did so with a perceived edge. Samuel had anointed him to be king (in time). When David saw the problem caused by the giant, he took charge of proceedings. His identity overshadowed what was impossible to everyone around him. He behaved like a king.

Power and authority come from within. The internal forces of our identity and our passion for God will overcome any external difficulties. Intimidation, stress and pressure always occupy the space between us and the crisis we face. Intimacy, peace and passion should always be our internal antidote. We never allow the battle to take place inside our heart. That is where identity reigns supreme. When he was taken before King Saul (1 Samuel 17:31–37) David's identity spoke to the king: "Let no man's heart fail on account of this giant, I will fight him."

It is our identity that pursues God. It explores His possibilities. Identity listens for the voice of God and only does what He says. Identity has a winning attitude. "I killed the lion and the bear, this uncircumcised Philistine shall be like one of those. The Lord will deliver me."

David took power with him onto the battlefield, but he also knew he was stepping into a power that the situation itself provided. Every crisis has power to overcome enshrined within it. Every adversarial situation contains power. We can either use that power to defeat the enemy or be used by it and be overcome. The internal power of our identity provides us with the confidence in God to discover and employ the external power that is provided by the circumstances.

Personal Notes

Who are you becoming? What is your current identity? Write it down here. Now, spend some time thinking about your present mindset about yourself. Then shift your thinking to the future. Who do you want to be? What is the stirring in your heart? Write down those thoughts and explore the meaning and the possibilities.

Every circumstance is loaded with upgrades

Our circumstances are not the problem. Our perception of our circumstances is the problem. We think of situations only in the context of the difficulties they contain. God sees them in the context of the provisions He has made available.

Every situation has opportunities for us to discover more about God and ourselves. The Lord never misses an opportunity to improve our spirituality and increase our identity. We are learning to be attuned to the voice of the Spirit of disclosure (John 16:13).

The circumstances we face can never just be about a situation being resolved. It must also be about us being changed. Some situations are a means to our growth personally. Others are about an increase of faith, authority or proclamation. Some are designed for us to capitalize on the fruit of the Spirit. Some teach us defensive warfare, others teach us offensive warfare. In defensive warfare we are learning how to stand and not get pushed around. We develop our capacity to keep our personal and home life free of attack. In offensive warfare we are looking for a fight. We intend to take ground or recover what has been lost or stolen.

Only the Holy Spirit knows the true purpose behind something. He knows the upgrades that are present and how to locate them. When our chief concern is rescue or resolution in the predicament, then we are never going to grow in the real stature in Christ. Upgrades come in all shapes and sizes. Some are incremental. They are small upgrades which are continuous over a period of time. Others are larger upgrades that happen more occasionally. Keep short accounts with the Holy Spirit. There is a general awareness of present disposition that comes with our relationship with a personal trainer. There are things we are working on now and other things that are programmed in for later.

What are you working on now in your character, faith, trust, intimacy and authority? What weights are you laying aside

(Hebrews 12:1)? What are you putting off and putting on in regard to your true self (Ephesians 4:22–24)?

I had a situation that was solely about an upgrade in patience. It ran for seven months. I stored up enough patience for a small company of people! Shortly afterwards I came into a circumstance that contained lots of conflict, opposition and personal attack. Here's the thing. It was the upgrade in patience that enabled me to take advantage in the warfare that surrounded me. Instead of becoming frustrated, angry, grieved and offended, I could practice love, grace and smiling. When the tempest blew out, I had new connections, more territory, and an increase in revenue.

Upgrades are present in all circumstances at all times. Sitting in my study, meditating on God's nature and giving thanks, I felt His Presence. I felt the sensation of warm oil being poured on my head. I kept lifting my hands to touch my hair, it was so real. I sat back and enjoyed it. Later, when I was processing it before the Lord, I felt Him say that my thinking had been upgraded. My capacity to know the mind of Christ had gone to another level. Over the next few months I tried out my upgrade in every situation and had a blast.

On another occasion in a worship service at The Mission I felt this incredible joy rise up within me. It would get to my mouth and just as I was about to laugh or shout for joy, it would subside. This happened seven times. I never got to express the joy externally in that meeting. Later I discovered that joy had gone into some deep places in my soul. I was carrying some wounds and disappointments and they healed up and changed. I could think differently about some people in that I could rejoice over them and see their future. Often we cannot see someone beyond the problem we are experiencing with them. In grace I was empowered to reconnect with them and share something that the Lord had shown me. It was a surprise and a blessing to them and opened up space for a conversation.

Personal Notes

What are the upgrades around you? What are you asking for currently? Look for it in the situations that you are facing. Make a list of the upgrades you need and the places where you need them. Expect the Lord to be faithful to you.

Do not live below your privilege!

You have a Divine Advantage. A relationship that provides astonishing benefits. You have a birthright. You have honor, favor and freedom. You have immunity, exemption and grace. You have patronage, indulgence and permission. You have Presence, power and authority. When we live in Christ, the Father endorses our circumstances.

Personal Notes

All of these are available to you in the Person of the Lord Jesus Christ. It is time to wake up to who you are and rise up to occupy your place. Apply your privilege to your circumstances. The biggest genius in the world will show you how. Ask the Holy Spirit. This, after all, is part of your training.

50

Relinquish the pain

We have all dealt or are dealing with issues of betrayal, disappointment and woundedness. In the future we will have situations that are unfair and hurtful. Prior to the resolution of these incidents is the small matter of our becoming Christlike.

The fruit of the Holy Spirit mostly grows in bad soil. How does kindness grow? It grows in the soil of a situation where someone has said or done something that is really unkind. Now we have a choice. Do we perform an act of kindness, say something generous? Or do we give like for like?

We hold on to the bad stuff. We use it to justify our position. Eventually it will take a heavier toll upon us than the original issue. As long as we have a hold on the pain and anger, we cannot progress. The trauma locks us into a present–past scenario and we are unable to move on. The wound will need more and more treatment the longer we allow it to continue.

A friend of mine in the British Army was wounded in a gun battle with insurgents. He was hit by a ricochet from a wall to his right. The surgeon recovered the bullet and closed the wound. However, there was a small fragment of stone that had entered just before the bullet. This remained inside and festered, requiring a second operation. He is OK now. It was very difficult for him until the wound was reopened and the foreign body eliminated.

The first step to recovery is the willingness to admit that we are sharing our heart with a foreign body that does not belong there. Then the hard step is to relinquish our pain and the justifications that have bound it to us. Let it go. Let it go. Speak it out every time the emotion rises up. "Lord, I relinquish this pain and anger to you. I let go of my justification and the need for vengeance. Take it out of my heart. I am done with it."

The next step is to renew your thinking so that those old thoughts can never return. When we want to deal with old thoughts we must think new ones first. It's a new for old policy in the Kingdom. We don't work on old mindsets — we just replace them. Like a light bulb. Take one out, put another in and switch on.

A part of that process is the need to forgive. Relinquish the blame that we put on ourselves or other people. When we really forgive people, we release any feeling that they owe us for the wrong done. We should be the ones to release the wrong. Set them free.

Holding onto a grudge means that we have made a decision to continue our own suffering. We have provided a safe harbor for our misery, grief, pain and anger. Resentment and bitterness will keep the grudge safe so that it can work its power on our hearts. The poison in our system can affect everyone around us. It creates an atmosphere that touches everyone around us, from the youngest to the eldest.

Relinquish the pain and start to live again.

Personal Notes

Write down the incident and what you feel about it. Put everything on paper so that you can handle this thing thoroughly. Write down what you need to do to recover yourself. Record what you need to do and say to set the other person(s) free. Make sure you are giving them full freedom.

51

When we give, we are being challenged to receive and move into fullness

We know that tithing is a tribute to the sovereignty of God. We give to Him in recognition of His majesty and His claim over us as loyal subjects. We give to Him also because we are in partnership with Him in the Kingdom. We believe that all we are and all we have belong to Him. We give because we are loved and this is part of the expression of our worship. We give because we want to put something in His hands for the work of the Kingdom, of which we are a vital part. We give because we cannot out-give God, for He is no man's debtor. We give because our giving is always overwhelmed by our receiving. We give as a hedge of protection around us. It is a safeguard against the devourer (Malachi 3:11) who loves to attack the economy of a nation, and the source of its wealth.

In our giving God receives from us the respect and awe that He deserves. He loves to be obligated in love. He loves to partner with us. He wishes to prosper us in all things (3 John 2) and our giving allows Him to do that. He loves to work with us, and giving puts us in a place of mutual resourcing; and He loves the greater part of that.

When we withhold our substance, it puts us in a place where we must at least become responsible for our own income. When we refuse to give, we are putting God behind us rather than in front of us. We are deducting the probability of increase. We are repressing the possibility of our prospering. We are on our own. We have resisted God's willingness to prosper us. We intend to battle the devourer by ourselves. We have suppressed blessing. By withholding, we are refusing God's input into our own personal economy. We relinquish His support when we make a go of it by ourselves.

If that was all we had to contend with then maybe we think we could handle it. However, it is a lot more personal than that to the Lord. He has given us so much already and for us not to reciprocate means that we come into deficit with Him. He calls withholding an act of robbery (Malachi 3:7–12) and commands that we return to Him in this regard.

The penalty for forsaking the Lord was laid down in the Old Testament (Deuteronomy 28:15–20). We come under a blight that affects all we have and do. We become vulnerable to the devourer. In the Old Testament, our disobedience carried with it a curse or a penalty. In the New Testament, Jesus took the curse upon Himself and paid the penalty. Therefore in the new covenant a penalty has become a consequence of behavior and not a curse. We will reap what we sow.

We cannot rob God of partnership and expect to receive when we need it. Our receiving can never overtake our withholding. When we fail to give, we put a cap on all that we have. We repress our own increase. We deduct blessing from ourselves.

When we lift the embargo on our giving, we remove the blockage from our receiving. Only God can rebuke the devourer for our sake. When we give, we put the Lord under a test of generosity. He says, "prove me now!" Only He can open windows of blessing until we overflow.

Only He would give us the challenge to receive. That is the partnership. Giving stimulates abundance. He wants us to give because then we become the ones challenged to receive. As Jesus put it: "Give and it shall be given to you. They will pour into your lap a good measure — pressed down, shaken together and running over. For by your standard of measure it will be measured to you in return." (Luke 6:38)

We are being measured for a blessing. It is in proportion to what we give. Our giving becomes our challenge to receive. The real challenge in our receiving is to move from lack into abundance. We are always being challenged by fullness. Ultimately, it is not about giving. It is about the need to be generous, open hearted and extravagant. When we give, we come into the realm of fullness, which changes our personality and makes us like God in our willingness to share and be generous. Generosity has already removed any possibility of anxiety. It looks to fullness alone as the source of life.

Personal Notes

If we do not tithe or give, we should read Malachi 3:7–12 and meditate on it. If we are consistent givers, then we must receive the challenge to be blessed. Ask and keep on asking. Consider too that this may be our moment to increase the stakes. Is God asking you to give more so that your partnership may increase?

Focus increases favor

It is important to pay attention to blessing. To live in a way that positions our life to receive from the Lord. We must concentrate on who Jesus is for us and know exactly what it means to be in Christ. Focus will always bring forth truth and power to bear on our circumstances. Focus allows us to pinpoint exactly where we need the favor of God to connect with our current situation. Effective prayer is never general. We pray with God, not towards Him. We pray in line with His will. Focus enables us to discover that will and speak it back to the Lord in the shared conversation. That is true prayer.

Favor is the intentional bias of God towards us. Focus on that bias! Think about it deeply (meditate). What does the Lord's patronage look like? We are a people who live under His smile. Focus enables us to receive under pressure. We live under God's approval because we are in Christ. Focus on the approval. The best prayers are fashioned out of the truth that God loves us to live in. What truth is the Father wanting you to embrace at this time? Focus on that! There is a prayer already waiting to be revealed. Focus will always increase your favor. Never allow your focus to be blurred.

Personal Notes

Concentrate your thinking on God's approval of you in Christ. Focus on your position in Jesus. What favor do you see? Zoom in on it and write it down. Make a prayer out of it; one that would make God smile and say yes!

52

An Appeal: Anti-Human Trafficking

William Wilberforce has long been one of my favorite heroes. He fought his own government and high society in an epic battle to abolish slavery. He succeeded admirably. In 1833, the British Parliament passed the Slavery Abolition Act which gave freedom to all slaves in the British Empire. Three decades later it also became law in the 13th Amendment to the U.S. Constitution.

Today slavery is back and worse than ever. The U.S. Secretary of State, Condoleeza Rice, states that, "defeating human trafficking is a great moral calling of our time." It is a huge business, profitable to the tune of over $30 billion. Almost 30 million people are enslaved by it. Most are children; millions are sex slaves.

We need to raise up a new generation of abolitionists that can counter a worldwide epidemic. Human trafficking is a criminal enterprise that is international. It is sophisticated in its corruptive influence on law enforcement and government officials across the globe.

More slaves are in bondage today than were sold in 400 years of the slave trade that was abolished in the 1800's. Slaves are disposable people — like batteries: once they exhaust their usefulness, they are replaced.

What is required is a relentless pursuit of justice — a refusal to accept a world where one individual can be held as the property of another. For more than three decades I have financed projects around the world aimed at relieving suffering and creating a better quality of life. Fighting against human trafficking is different. It is not a project; it's more of a crusade. I want to affect things at a high level as well as on the ground.

I have a separate account within the ministry where I am setting aside a percentage of profits from all our endeavors to give into this worthy cause. Join us as the Lord leads you, or get involved some way yourself. Do something!

If you wish to donate with your order through Brilliant Book House (please be advised that we are a for-profit company), then send your gift with the notation "Not For Sale" to:

Brilliant Book House
865 Cotting Ln, Ste C
Vacaville, CA 95688

Alternatively, if you want a tax credit for your gift, more information and a chance to donate can be found at this website: www.notforsalecampaign.org.

Checks can be made payable to Not for Sale:

270 Capistrano Road, Ste #2
Half Moon Bay, CA 94019

Phone: (650) 560-9990
www.notforsalecampaign.org

With heartfelt thanks,
Graham Cooke

Other Books by Graham Cooke

- ~: A Divine Confrontation... Birth Pangs of the New Church
- ~: Developing Your Prophetic Gifting (Outdated and now out-of-print. It is being replaced by The Prophetic Equipping Series Volumes 1 – 6
- ~: Permission Granted (co-authored)

The Prophetic Equipping Series:
- ~: Volume 1–Approaching the Heart of Prophecy
- ~: Volume 2–Prophecy and Responsibility
- ~: Volume 3–Prophetic Wisdom

The Being With God Series:
- ~: The Nature of God
- ~: Hiddenness and Manifestation
- ~: Crafted Prayer
- ~: Beholding and Becoming
- ~: Toward a Powerful Inner Life
- ~: The Language of Promise
- ~: God's Keeping Power
- ~: Living in Dependency and Wonder

The Way of the Warrior Series:
- ~: Volume 1 – Qualities of a Spiritual Warrior
- ~: Volume 2 – Manifesting Your Spirit
- ~: Volume 3 – Coming into Alignment

The Wisdom Series:
- ~: Secret Sayings, Hidden Meanings
- ~: Radical Perceptions

About the Author

Graham Cooke is part of The Mission's core leadership team, working with senior team leader, David Crone, in Vacaville, California. Graham's role includes training, consulting, mentoring and being part of a think tank that examines the journey from present to future.

He is married to Theresa, who has a passion for worship and dance. She loves to be involved in intercession, warfare, and setting people free. She cares about injustice and abuse, and has compassion on people who are sick, suffering and disenfranchised.

They have six children and three grandchildren. Ben and Seth both reside and work in the UK. Ben is developing as a writer, is very funny, and probably knows every movie ever made. Seth is a musician, a deep thinker with a caring outlook and an amazing capacity for mischief. Seth is married to Sara, a lovable, intelligent and very funny girl.

Sophie and her husband Mark live in Vacaville and attend The Mission. Sophie & Mark are the Operations Managers of Brilliant Book House, the publishing company of Graham Cooke. Sophie has played a significant part in Graham's ministry for a number of years, and has helped develop resources, new books and journals, as well as organize events. Mark and Sophie are a warm-hearted, friendly, deeply humorous couple with lots of friends. Mark and Sophie have two daughters. Evelyn (August 2006) is a delight; a happy little soul who likes music, loves to dance and enjoys books. Annabelle (December 2008) is loud, funny, determined and unafraid. Granddaughter #3 is due any day and the name is a secret.

Their other daughters are Alexis, who is loving, kind and gentle, and very intuitive and steadfast toward her friends; and Alyssa, a very focused and determined young woman who is fun-loving with a witty sense of humor.

Also, Graham and Theresa have two beautiful young women, Julianne and Megan, both in Australia, who are a part of their extended family.

Graham is a popular conference speaker and is well known for his training programs on the prophetic, spiritual warfare, intimacy and devotional life, leadership, spirituality and the church in transition. He functions as a consultant and freethinker to businesses, churches, and organizations, enabling them to develop strategically. He has a passion to establish the Kingdom and build prototype churches that can fully reach a post-modern society.

A strong part of Graham's ministry is in producing finances and resources to the poor and disenfranchised in developing countries. He supports many projects specifically for widows, orphans and people in the penal system. He hates abuse of women and works actively against human trafficking and the sex slave trade, including women caught up in prostitution and pornography.

If you would like to invite Graham to minister or speak at an event, please complete the online Ministry Invitation Form at www.GrahamCooke.com.

If you wish to become a financial partner for the sake of missions and compassionate acts across the nations, please contact his office at office@myemerginglight.com, and his administrative assistant will be happy to assist you.

You may contact Graham by writing to:
Graham Cooke
865 Cotting Lane, Ste C
Vacaville, California
95688, USA

www.GrahamCooke.com

Brilliant Book House

Brilliant Book House is a California-based publishing company founded and directed by Graham Cooke and is dedicated to producing high-quality Christian resources and teaching materials. Brilliant Book House seeks to equip all of our readers to lead brilliant lives, confidently led by the Holy Spirit into the destiny God has for you.

We believe you have a unique call on your life that can only be found in God. He has something for you that is far beyond your wildest dreams. As you step out into that purpose, we want to stand with you, offering you encouragement, training, and hope for your journey. We want to equip you for what God wants to do in you, and through you. That is our promise to you.

Brilliant is the culmination of a longtime dream of our founder, Graham Cooke. A thinker and a strategist, Graham is also a builder with a particular desire to establish resource churches that are prophetic, progressive, and supernatural. Brilliant Book House is a key part of that call, producing books, journals, MP3s, e-books, DVDs, CDs, and other teaching materials. For more on Graham, please visit www.brilliantbookhouse.com.